RACHAEL RAY
EXPRESS LANE
MEALS

another 30-minute meal cookbook!

CHILI PEPPER
MCC THYME LV
MCC BLK PEPR
MCC GRLC PPR
MCC OREGANO
MCCORMICK
MCC BAY LVES
MCC CINN GRD
MCC FENEL SD
MCC RED PEPR
1.29

OSCR ANCHVIE

RACHAEL RAY
EXPRESS LANE
MEALS

What to Keep on Hand, What to Buy Fresh
for the Easiest-Ever 30-Minute Meals

Clarkson Potter/Publishers
New York

All rights reserved.
Published in the United States by Clarkson
Potter/Publishers, an imprint of the Crown
Publishing Group, a division of Random
House, Inc., New York.
www.crownpublishing.com
www.clarksonpotter.com

Clarkson N. Potter is a trademark and Potter
and colophon are registered trademarks of
Random House, Inc.

Library of Congress Cataloging-in-
Publication Data
is available upon request

ISBN-13: 978-1-4000-8255-1

ISBN-10: 1-4000-8255-2

Printed in the United States of America

Design by Jennifer K. Beal

10 9 8

First Edition

Thanks

To all the Express Lane checkers at markets
everywhere who are underappreciated by
their overtired customers. We are not
always nice to you, and I for one want to
offer a collective thank-you for getting
us to our food faster! We, your customers,
are nicer once fed.

As always, thanks to good eaters
everywhere, fans of *30-Minute Meals,* my
coworkers at my many jobs, my friends,
my family, and all our sweet animals. You
make my life and my work a true joy and
very delicious!

.29

OSCR ANCHVI

0.89

BUSH GARBAN

REGINA VING

HNZ-CIDR VI

MON VINEGAR

PEPFRM MUFF

CARROTS 40

Contents

CARROTS 4094
POLAND WATER
2 @ 3.49
MSHRM P/C704
2 @ 1.99
ITLN BASIL
2 @ 4.99
GAB IMP ROM
2 @ 3.99
POLATO E4732
2 @ 1.99
GRPE TOMATO

Introduction

I am asked often about what I keep in my kitchen to have on hand at all times. I am also often asked what everyone *else* should keep on hand in their own kitchens. Answering the first question is pretty easy: pasta, EVOO, tomatoes, canned beans, cheese, salami, and the like. That second question, though, always throws me for a loop! If I don't answer I feel as if people might get the impression I don't care; by answering it too specifically, I might sound like I know what you like to eat better than you do! Messy question, indeed.

I get off the hook by answering as diplomatically as I can. "It depends on what style of food you enjoy most. If you love Tex-Mex and spicy food, keep lots of beans, tomatoes, dried ground cumin, chili powders, and canned chili peppers on hand. If you love Italian, go for pastas and grains, tomatoes, EVOO, and balsamic vinegar."

Boy, did I fix my red wagon! Now people have started asking for the details: Which kinds of beans? How many cans of tomatoes? Well, I am going to give it a shot!

This book contains a list of around seventy items that I *always* have on hand in either the spice rack, fridge, freezer, or cupboard. It is based on a mixed bag of cooking styles: Mediterranean, Mexican and Spanish, Continental or Bistro, Asian, and American. If you build this On-Hand list and restock the list every two weeks or so, then you can make any of the recipes that follow with the addition of no more than ten items from the market, ensuring yourself a perpetual spot on the Express Lane! I'm not suggesting you go out and buy every item on this list all at once, but rather that you accumulate them over time. Most of the items are non-perishable or frozen, so once you've made the investment it will pay dividends for many months of meals.

This book is a true reflection of how I live my day-to-day life. I do a BIG shop every couple of weeks and pick up a few fill-in items or entrée basics each day I cook. I cook a lot because the system works and always keeps me in groceries. Best of all, even if I am super tired, I always have the security blanket of knowing I can go straight home and cook something groovy right from my cupboard.

Happy stocking up, and good eating!

2 @ 1.99

ONIONS 004

1.49 lb @ 3.99 /lb

NT   GARLIC 4608

3 @ 4.49

GOYA CHORIZC

BUSH CANNELL

2 @ 0.89

BUSH BEANS

B&G PEPPERS

MCILHEN TBSC

L&P SAUCE

Rachael's Top 5 Tips for Grocery Shopping Like a Pro

Unit Price

Always look at the unit price (generally noted as price per ounce, either fluid or weight) rather than the sticker price when you are selecting an item. You'll find the unit price on the shelf label to the left of the item's sticker price. It gives you the value of the grocery item and it is the only true way to compare costs between different brands and package sizes. This way you'll know the actual price of your EVOO, stock, tomatoes, et cetera.

Stocking Up

When you see a sale on a pricey item like chicken breasts or filet mignon, buy more than you need for your meal and freeze the extras in small portions. Place the chicken breasts in small freezer bags with a splash of water and pound them out into cutlets, then place them in the freezer. When frozen solid you can stack them to save space. Cut a large piece of filet into small tournedos (1-inch-thick steaks), and wrap them in parchment paper, and then place them in freezer bags in single-serve portions. Salmon is on sale? Buy a whole side and cut it into 6-ounce fillets, then individually sack 'em and stack 'em! This way you always have go-to versatile, high-quality entrée choices in single or multiple servings. The small portions also defrost quickly.

Time Is Money. What's Your Time Worth?

If you need to get the food on the table fast, take a little help on the prep work. In the fresh produce department I will often pick up raw trimmed green beans or shredded carrots or cabbage. I even pick up whole boiled eggs from the salad bar when I want to use them for a salad garnish.

Many Trips Make Small Work

Once you've built up your on-hand goods, keep it up with biweekly big shops. Every other week hit the market hard with your master list of staples. Use the list in this book or download a list you can customize from www.clarksonpotter.com to reflect the staples *you* use most often in your kitchen. During the workweek, all you'll need are fresh meats and fill-in ingredients, which you can pick up every couple of nights, helping you become a frequent traveler through the Express Lane!

Put It Away Clean!

When you bring home your groceries, wash all the greens, herbs, and veggies, dry them, and put them away in plastic food storage bags. The herbs especially will keep up to 2 weeks once trimmed, plus you will save time every night because your ingredients will be ready and waiting for you to use—no stopping to spin lettuce or rinse parsley.

Swap Meet

Burgers and sammies of all descriptions have to be at the very top of my list for dinner on those nights when I'm *almost* too tired to cook. Nine times out of ten I just add a handful of chips—good quality, well-seasoned, thick-sliced chips like Terra's Yukon Golds—to the plate and I'm done. Chips not your bag? Substitute one of the following based on what you have on hand and how much extra energy you have:

❑ Raw veggies. Buy them right off the salad bar or use whatever you've got in the fridge, and think sugar-snap peas, trimmed green beans, sliced bell peppers and fennel, or cherry tomatoes in addition to the same old carrots and celery sticks;

❑ Tossed green salad (buy washed baby greens in a sack) topped with one or all of the following: canned chickpeas, halved grape tomatoes, and/or black olives in a simple EVOO-and-red-wine vinegar dressing;

❑ Doctor prepared hummus with a squeeze of lemon juice and a chopped roasted red pepper and serve with cucumber chips or celery dippers;

❑ Mix any leftover cooked vegetables—chopped green beans or broccoli, corn, peas—with a drained can of black beans. Dress with EVOO and a good squeeze of lime juice plus a pinch of cumin and salt (throw in some chopped cilantro if you have it and want to get fancy);

❑ Stir together thinly sliced cucumbers and onions with sour cream or yogurt; add a splash of vinegar and a pinch of salt and sugar.

Keep It On Hand: The Master List of What to Buy, How Much to Keep Around, and Where to Store It

These are the basics that you should have on hand at all times—not just what to buy but how much and where to store it. Restock these items every two weeks, (keep the cheat sheet from the back flap of this book with you when you do a big shop as a reminder). Use the Express Lane shopping lists at the back of the book for quick, end-of-day shops. You can also note any staples you may need to replenish mid-week there as well.

Note: Most spices and seasonings are available in small, square metal tins, glass jars, and small plastic bottles—any and all of which I think of as a single "unit." Buy spices in the smallest units you can find and toss whatever you haven't used after 6 months or so for the freshest flavor. The exceptions are salt and pepper, which you can buy in larger quantities because you will go through them quickly and should never run out!

In the Spice Rack

❑ coarse salt	1 large unit, 26 ounces or more	❑ curry paste or powder	1 unit
		❑ ground coriander	1 unit
❑ coarse black pepper or peppercorns to grind	1 large unit	❑ poultry seasoning	1 unit
		❑ bay leaves	1 unit
		❑ red pepper flakes	1 unit
❑ chili powder	1 unit	❑ dried oregano	1 unit
❑ ground cumin	1 unit	❑ dried thyme	1 unit
❑ grill seasoning	1 large unit	❑ ground cinnamon	1 unit
❑ paprika	1 unit	❑ fennel seeds	1 unit
❑ smoked sweet paprika	1 unit	❑ ground allspice	1 unit
		❑ cayenne pepper	1 unit
❑ whole nutmeg	1 unit		

In the Fridge

❏ milk	2 quarts
❏ heavy cream or half-and-half	1 quart
❏ butter	1 pound unless it's on sale and then you should buy a backup to keep in the freezer
❏ eggs	1 dozen
❏ Parmigiano-Reggiano	1-pound cut of Parm
❏ Pecorino Romano	1 large tub of freshly grated Pecorino Romano
❏ bacon	1 pound unless it's on sale and then you should buy a backup to keep in the freezer
❏ hot sauce	1 6-ounce bottle
❏ Dijon mustard	1 jar (8 to 10 ounces)
❏ spicy brown mustard	1 jar (8 to 10 ounces)
❏ capers	1 jar
❏ flat-leaf parsley	2 bunches washed and dried, in food storage bags
❏ celery	1 bunch
❏ carrots	1 pound
❏ mayonnaise	1 small jar (8 ounces)

In the Freezer

❏ frozen peas	2 10-ounce boxes
❏ frozen corn	2 10-ounce boxes
❏ frozen chopped spinach	2 10-ounce boxes
❏ plain and Italian bread crumbs	1 15-ounce container each

Somewhere in the Kitchen

❏ Idaho potatoes	5 pounds
❏ small red, baby Yukon Gold, or small white boiling potatoes	5 pounds
❏ lemons	6
❏ limes	6
❏ Spanish or yellow onions	4-pound sack
❏ shallots	4 large
❏ peanut butter, chunky or smooth	1 jar
❏ garlic	4 heads

In the Wine Rack

❏ white wine	2 bottles
❏ red wine	2 bottles
❏ dry sherry	1 bottle

In the Cupboard

❑ chicken stock in a box	3 32-ounce cartons
❑ beef stock in a box	2 32-ounce cartons
❑ diced fire-roasted tomatoes	2 14-ounce cans
❑ diced tomatoes (regular and petite-diced)	1 14-ounce can each
❑ crushed tomatoes	3 28-ounce cans
❑ tomato paste	1 tube or small can
❑ tomato sauce	2 8-ounce cans
❑ chipotle chilies in adobo or dry chipotle powder	1 small can or jar
❑ black beans	2 14-ounce cans
❑ chickpeas/garbanzo beans	2 14-ounce cans
❑ cannellini beans	2 14-ounce cans
❑ long-cut pastas such as spaghetti, linguine, vermicelli, angel hair, and fettuccine	4 pounds, different varieties
❑ short-cut pastas such as penne, ditalini, gemelli, and cavatappi	4 pounds, different varieties

❑ plain couscous	2 6-ounce boxes
❑ white rice	1 5-pound sack
❑ all-purpose flour	1 2-pound sack
❑ white sugar	1 2-pound box
❑ brown sugar	1 pound box
❑ Italian tuna in EVOO	2 4-ounce cans
❑ tuna in water	2 6-ounce cans
❑ Alaskan salmon	1 14.75-ounce can
❑ Worcestershire sauce	1 10-ounce bottle
❑ vegetable oil	1 48-ounce bottle
❑ tamari	1 bottle
❑ balsamic vinegar	1 bottle
❑ red wine vinegar	1 bottle
❑ cider, white wine and/or rice vinegar	1 bottle
❑ honey	1 small jar
❑ EVOO	2 large bottles (whatever the bargain is)
❑ anchovy fillets	2 tins or 1 small jar
❑ roasted red peppers in water	1 16-ounce jar
❑ canned clams, whole baby	2 14-ounce cans

Drunken Tuscan Pasta 202

**Bacon and Creamy Ranch Chicken Burgers
with Crispy Scallion "Sticks" 236**

**Hungry Man Bloody-Mary Burgers with Spicy
Garlic-Roasted Broccoli 66**

Spanish Pork Chops with Linguica Corn Stuffing,
Cherry-Red Wine Gravy, and Steamed Green Beans 206

Thai Chicken Pizza   142

Steaks with Tangy Corn Relish and Super Cheese and Scallion Smashed Spuds   168

Montalcino Chicken with Figs and Buttered Gnocchi
with Nutmeg   238

RACHAEL RAY
EXPRESS LANE
MEALS

L&P SAUCE
TUT NW CRSH
4C PLN CRMBS
BE SWT CORN
2 @ 1.69
CELERY   4070
0.92 lb @ 1.99 /lb
T   SW CHARD4586
2 @ 1.99
BROCOLI 4060
DILL   4891
2 @ 1.99

MEALS FOR THE EXHAUSTED

Here is a whole bunch of recipes for those nights when you are most likely to call for take-out (hey, sometimes I do, too). I group these recipes together because they require the least amount of brain power and physical effort. You may find recipes in other sections made entirely from your "On Hand" ingredients, whereas there *are* short Express Lane lists throughout this section. Don't let that stop you; these remain the simplest dinners to put together, period. I did leave out a few of my "I'm exhausted" fallbacks, like Grape-Nuts with Milk and Grilled Swiss and Tomato on Rye and the ever-popular "Raid the Deli Tubs and Glass Jars in Your Fridge" because none of these needs a recipe. However, there are some real surprises in here, including easy, elegant, bistro fare for last-minute date nights such as Sexy Surf and Turf. Some personal favorites: Spaghetti alla Ceci and Three-Vegetable Penne with Tarragon-Basil Pesto, 'cause I love pasta . . . especially when I'm tired. The carbs send me off into a blissful food coma.

Inside-out Pizza-dilla Margerita

Take a pizza Margerita, make it on a tortilla, then fold it like a quesadilla and you get a pizza-dilla!

4 SERVINGS

1 tablespoon **EVOO** (extra-virgin olive oil), once around the pan, plus more for drizzling

2 **garlic cloves**, chopped

2 pinches **red pepper flakes**

1 15-ounce can diced **fire-roasted tomatoes**, drained

¼ teaspoon, a couple of pinches, **dried oregano**

Salt and **black pepper**

8 8-inch **flour tortillas**

1-pound ball **smoked mozzarella** cheese, thinly sliced

1 cup fresh **basil**, about 20 leaves, torn or shredded

Heat a small skillet over medium heat. Add the tablespoon of EVOO to the skillet, once around the pan. Add the garlic and red pepper flakes. Cook the garlic for a minute, then add the tomatoes and season with oregano, salt, and pepper. Simmer the tomatoes for 2 minutes, then remove from the heat.

Heat a medium skillet over medium heat. Add a drizzle of EVOO and a flour tortilla. Cover the tortilla with an even layer of sliced cheese. Top it with one quarter of the tomatoes. Scatter one quarter of the basil over the tomatoes. Set a second tortilla in place on top. Cook it for 2 minutes on side one, drizzle the top of the tortilla with a touch of EVOO, and flip the pizza-dilla. Cook for 2 minutes more, or until golden and crisp on the flip side. Remove, cut into 4 pieces, and serve. Repeat this with the remaining ingredients to make 3 more pizza-dillas.

EXPRESS LANE
SHOPPING LIST

❑ 1 package 8-inch flour
   tortillas

❑ 1-pound ball smoked
   mozzarella

❑ 1 bunch fresh basil

And make sure you have
the following On Hand:

EVOO • Garlic • Red pepper
flakes • Canned diced
fire-roasted tomatoes •
Dried oregano • Salt and
black pepper

Leek-y Chicken and Couscous

About ten years ago, my friend Donna told me she had made chicken with leeks—just leeks—for dinner the night before and she raved about it! I made my own version of Leek-y Chicken that night and I've been making it ever since. I included a version of this recipe in my first 30-Minute cookbook back in 1998, but I could not do a book on "Express" cooking without including Leek-y Chicken in some form. Here it is served on a bed of couscous.

4 SERVINGS

1½ cups **chicken stock**

2 tablespoons **butter**

¼ cup **golden raisins**, a couple of handfuls, chopped

1½ cups plain **couscous**

2 tablespoons **EVOO** (extra-virgin olive oil), twice around the pan

1½ pounds **chicken tenders**, cut into large bite-size pieces

Salt and **black pepper**

2 medium **leeks** or 1 large leek

1 cup **dry white wine** (eyeball it), about ¼ bottle

A handful of fresh **flat-leaf parsley**, chopped

Heat the chicken stock and 1 tablespoon of the butter in a medium pot with a tight-fitting lid. When the liquid boils, add the raisins and couscous. Take the pan off the heat. Stir the couscous and place the lid on the pot. Let it stand.

Heat a large nonstick skillet over medium-high heat and add the EVOO. Add the chicken in a single layer and season it with salt and pepper. While the chicken browns on all sides, trim the rough tops and the root ends off the leeks.

Cut the leeks in half lengthwise, then cut them into 1-inch half moons. Place the leeks in a colander and run them under cold water. Separate the layers to release the dirt and grit. Rinse well, then drain well.

Add the leeks to the chicken and wilt, 2 to 3 minutes. Add the wine and let it cook down by half, 3 to 4 minutes. The leeks should still have some color but should be tender and the chicken should be cooked through. Add the remaining tablespoon of butter and swirl into the sauce.

Fluff the couscous with a fork and stir in the parsley. Place a bed of couscous on each dinner plate and top it with the chicken and leeks.

EXPRESS LANE SHOPPING LIST

- **Small box** golden raisins (snack size is ok)
- **1½ pounds** chicken tenders
- **2 medium** leeks or 1 large leek

And make sure you have the following On Hand:

Chicken stock • Butter • Plain couscous • EVOO • Salt and black pepper • Dry white wine • Flat-leaf parsley

Spaghetti alla Ceci

Ceci are chickpeas. This is a classic, simple Italian dinner. Thousands of tired Romans will be eating it tonight; how about we join them? Greens dressed with vinegar and oil would make a good side dish.

4 SERVINGS

Salt

1 pound spaghetti

3 tablespoons EVOO (extra-virgin olive oil), 3 times around the pan

1/2 teaspoon red pepper flakes

3 to 4 garlic cloves, finely chopped

1 14-ounce can chickpeas, drained

1/2 teaspoon dried thyme (eyeball it)

Black pepper

1/2 cup dry white wine or chicken stock

1 14-ounce can crushed tomatoes

A handful of fresh flat-leaf parsley, chopped

Grated Parmigiano-Reggiano cheese, to pass at the table

Bring a big pot of water to a boil for the pasta. Salt it and cook the spaghetti to al dente.

While the spaghetti cooks, heat a large skillet over medium heat. Add the EVOO, red pepper flakes, and garlic. Place the chickpeas in a food processor and pulse to a fine chop. Add the chickpeas to the skillet with the garlic and season them with the thyme, salt, and pepper. Sauté them for 3 to 4 minutes. Add the wine or stock and cook down for 30 seconds or so, then stir in the tomatoes and adjust the seasoning. Drain the pasta and toss with the sauce. Top the pasta with the parsley and grated cheese.

Canadian Benny's

Recently I went with some close girlfriends to Nova Scotia. There's a lot more than lox going on up there! At the Normaway Inn on Cape Breton Island our favorite meal was brunch; this is my version of their Eggs Benedict. It's good for B, L, or D—breakfast, lunch, or dinner!

4 SERVINGS

4   tablespoons (½ stick) **butter**

2   **plum tomatoes**, seeded and chopped

2   **scallions**, finely chopped

   Salt and **black pepper**

1   cup **heavy cream**

4   thick-cut slices sweet, **whole-grain bread**

   A drizzle of **EVOO** (extra-virgin olive oil)

8   slices **Canadian bacon**

4   large **eggs**

8   ounces sharp **Canadian Cheddar** cheese, sliced or shredded

Melt 1 tablespoon of the butter over medium heat in a small pan. Add the tomatoes and scallions and season with salt and pepper. Sauté for 2 minutes, then stir in the cream and let it reduce for 10 minutes over low heat, stirring occasionally.

Heat a large nonstick skillet over medium heat. Add 2 tablespoons of butter to the skillet and melt it. Add the bread slices and cook for 3 to 4 minutes on each side. Transfer the slices to a platter. Add a drizzle of EVOO to the same pan and cook the Canadian bacon for 2 to 3 minutes on each side. Place 2 slices of bacon on each slice of bread.

Add the remaining tablespoon of butter to the pan. When it has melted, carefully add the eggs, giving each room to cook. Fry over soft or hard, as you like. Cover the eggs with mounds of cheese. Tent the pan in foil to melt the cheese. Place each cheesy egg on a bacon-topped slice of bread. Ladle the tomato cream sauce over each stack. Eggcellent, eh?

EXPRESS LANE
SHOPPING LIST

❑ **2** plum tomatoes
❑ **1 bunch** scallions
❑ **1 loaf** sweet, whole-grain bread, **such as oat-nut**
❑ **8 slices** Canadian bacon (about ½ pound)
❑ **8 ounces sharp** Canadian Cheddar **cheese**

And make sure you have the following On Hand:

Butter • Salt and black pepper • Heavy cream • EVOO • Eggs

Mighty Migas
Huevos with Cajones!

This one is a B, L, D: good for breakfast, lunch, or dinner. It's easy to adjust to make a single serving; I often opt for eggs if I am cooking for just myself. *Migas* in soft tortillas is a favorite dish in Austin, Texas, and now it's a favorite of mine. When I am home alone I put Bob Schneider, my favorite Austin musician, on my stereo and invite him to sit down to share my *migas*. I end up eating his, since my imaginary boyfriends eat light!

4 SERVINGS

- 3 tablespoons **EVOO** (extra-virgin olive oil), 3 times around the pan
- 2 **jalapeño peppers**, seeded and chopped
- 1 small red or green **bell pepper**, cored, seeded, and chopped
- 1 small **white onion**, chopped

  Salt and **black pepper**
- 2 **plum tomatoes**, seeded and diced
- 8 large **eggs**, beaten
- 1 cup crushed **tortilla chips**
- 1 10-ounce sack (2 cups) shredded **Monterey Jack** or Cheddar cheese
- 8 6-inch **flour tortillas** (soft taco size)
- 1 cup **tomato sauce**
- 1 to 2 **chipotle chilies in adobo**, medium to extra hot, finely chopped

  A handful of fresh **cilantro**, finely chopped

Heat a large skillet over medium-high heat. Add the EVOO. Add the jalapeños, bell peppers, and onions and season them with salt and pepper. Cook for 2 to 3 minutes, then add the tomatoes and cook a minute more. Beat the eggs with a pinch of salt and pepper and add to the veggies. Reduce the heat to medium low. Scramble the eggs not quite halfway, so they are still nice and wet. Add the crushed tortilla chips and scramble them in. Cover the eggs with the cheese and turn off the heat. Cover the pan loosely with foil to melt the cheese and set aside for a minute.

Heat a second, dry skillet over high heat. Add the tortillas one at a time and sear for 30 seconds on each side to blister them.

In a small bowl, stir together the tomato sauce and the chopped chipotle. Stir in the cilantro.

Place a mound of the *migas* on each flour tortilla and dot with the sauce. Serve immediately, two per person.

Cacio e Pepe (Cheese and Pepper Pasta) and Spinach with White Beans

This Roman dish is as old as the city's seven hills. It doesn't get any easier, really. As a side, I fry up some garlic in oil and toss it with chopped defrosted spinach and some rinsed canned white beans.

4 SERVINGS

Salt

1 pound **spaghetti**

3 tablespoons **butter**, cut into small pieces

5 tablespoons **EVOO** (extra-virgin olive oil)

2 teaspoons **coarse black pepper**

1 cup grated **Pecorino Romano** cheese, 3 rounded handfuls

1 10-ounce box chopped **frozen spinach**

3 to 4 **garlic cloves**, chopped

1 14-ounce can **cannellini beans**, rinsed and drained

¼ teaspoon freshly grated **nutmeg**

Bring a large pot of water to a boil for the pasta and salt it. Add the pasta and cook to al dente. Heads up: you'll need to use a ladle of the cooking water (about ¼ cup) for the sauce right before you drain the pasta.

Place a large skillet over low heat with the butter, 1 tablespoon of the EVOO, and pepper. Let it hang out until the pasta is done.

When the pasta is ready, take a ladle of the starchy cooking water and add it to the butter-pepper mixture. Drain the pasta and toss it in the pan with the sauce. Turn off the heat. Add the cheese in small handfuls, then toss the pasta with tongs, until all the cheese is incorporated into the creamy sauce. Add another ladle of cooking water if needed, then season the pasta to taste with salt and drizzle with 2 tablespoons of the EVOO.

While the pasta works, defrost the spinach in the microwave for 6 minutes on high. Place the spinach in a clean kitchen towel and wring the water out. Heat a small skillet over medium heat. Add the remaining 2 tablespoons of EVOO, twice around the pan, then the garlic. Cook the garlic for 2 minutes, and then add the beans. Add the spinach to the beans, breaking it up as you drop it into the pan. Season the spinach and beans with nutmeg, salt, and pepper. Serve the spinach and beans alongside the hot pasta.

And make sure you have the following On Hand:

Salt • Spaghetti • Butter • EVOO • Black pepper • Pecorino Romano cheese • Frozen chopped spinach • Garlic • Canned cannellini beans • Nutmeg

Linguine with Rach's Cupboard Red Clam Sauce

Anchovies work magic here. Once they melt they will not taste fishy; they'll taste more like salted nuts, really. Plus, anchovies in any seafood sauce I serve are the secret ingredient that makes the eaters go "Hmm, what is that?" (Don't tell anyone my secret, k?)

4 SERVINGS

Salt

1 pound linguine

3 tablespoons EVOO (extra-virgin olive oil), 3 times around the pan

1 tin flat anchovy fillets, 2 ounces, drained

½ teaspoon red pepper flakes (eyeball it in your palm)

¼ teaspoon dried oregano leaves, a couple of pinches

1 teaspoon dried thyme leaves, ⅓ palmful

5 to 6 garlic cloves, finely chopped

1 small onion, finely chopped

½ cup dry red wine, a couple of glugs

2 14-ounce cans whole baby clams in juice

1 28-ounce can crushed tomatoes

Black pepper

2 handfuls of chopped fresh flat-leaf parsley

Lemon zest, for garnish

Bring a large pot of water to a boil for the pasta. Salt the water, add the pasta, and cook to al dente.

Heat a large, deep skillet over medium-low heat. Add the EVOO, then add the anchovies and melt them into the oil. Next, add the red pepper flakes, oregano, thyme, and garlic. Cook the garlic for a minute, then add the onions, raise the heat to medium, and cook, stirring frequently, for 3 to 4 minutes, until the onions begin to get soft. Add the wine and cook it for a minute, then stir in the clams, adding the juice from one can (drain the other before you add the clams). Stir to combine and cook down the juice a minute or so to concentrate the flavor. Stir in the crushed tomatoes and season with salt and pepper (there's so much anchovy and clam in this sauce you may not need salt at all—taste to test it).

Drain the linguine well and add it to the sauce in the skillet. Add half the parsley and toss the pasta with the sauce. Adjust the salt and pepper and plate the pasta, garnishing it with the extra parsley and a little lemon zest.

And make sure you have the following On Hand:

Salt • Linguine • EVOO • Anchovy fillets • Red pepper flakes • Dried oregano • Dried thyme • Garlic • Onion • Dry red wine • Canned whole baby clams in juice • Canned crushed tomatoes • Black pepper • Flat-leaf parsley • Lemon

Sexy Surf and Turf
Seared Scallops and Tenderloin Steaks
with Manhattan Sauce

I came up with this one because we always have sweet vermouth on hand to make Manhattans, but we use it for nothing else. It's a big bottle. This sauce is so good that we may actually need to get another bottle one day soon!

(Who knew you could make such a sexy meal so simply? Hey, there are some things you should never be too tired for, wink-wink, nudge-nudge!)

4 SERVINGS

EVOO (extra-virgin olive oil), for drizzling, plus 1 tablespoon, once around the pan

4 **tenderloin steaks**, 1 inch thick

8 large **diver sea scallops**

Salt and **black pepper**

1 large **shallot**, chopped

2 **garlic cloves**, chopped

¼ cup **sweet vermouth** (but if you drink Manhattans, you've got this On Hand!)

2 tablespoons **butter**

1 pound thin **asparagus**, tough ends trimmed

Juice of ½ lemon

2 tablespoons chopped or snipped **chives**, 10 blades, for garnish

> **TIDBIT**
> Your scallops may still have the adductor muscle—a thin, tough strip that attaches the animal to its shell—intact. If so, nick it off with your fingers.

EXPRESS LANE
SHOPPING LIST

❑ 4 inch-thick tenderloin
   steaks
❑ 8 large diver sea scallops
❑ 1 pound thin asparagus
❑ 1 bunch fresh chives

LIQUOR STORE

❑ ¼ cup sweet vermouth
   (but if you drink
   Manhattans, you've got
   this On Hand!)

Drizzle some EVOO over the steaks to coat them lightly. Get a nonstick skillet screaming hot and add the meat. Cook for 3 minutes on each side for medium rare, 4 for medium to medium well. Transfer the steaks to a platter and pull the pan off the heat to cool for a minute.

Pat the scallops completely dry. Drizzle some EVOO over the scallops and season them with salt and pepper. Get a skillet screaming hot and cook the scallops for 2 to 3 minutes on each side, until they are well caramelized.

Bring 2 inches of water to a boil in a clean medium skillet for the asparagus.

Return the pan you cooked the meat in to the stove over medium heat and add 1 tablespoon of EVOO, once around the pan. Add the shallots and garlic and cook for 2 minutes. Add the sweet vermouth and cook until reduced by half, 30 seconds or so. Add the butter to the pan and swirl to incorporate to finish the sauce.

Add the asparagus to the boiling water. Cook for 2 to 3 minutes, or until just tender and bright green. Remove to a plate and dress the asparagus with the lemon juice, a drizzle of EVOO, and salt and pepper.

Place each tenderloin steak on a plate and drizzle the Manhattan sauce over the top. Arrange 2 scallops on top of each steak and garnish with the chives. Serve the asparagus spears alongside.

And make sure you have the following On Hand:

EVOO • Salt and black pepper • Shallot • Garlic • Butter • Lemon

Three-Vegetable Penne with Tarragon-Basil Pesto

With veggies and pasta in one dish, there's no need to make any sides—plus, you only have to wash one pot!

4 SERVINGS

    Salt

1 pound **penne rigate** (ridged) pasta

½ pound **asparagus**, tough ends trimmed

1 small **zucchini**

¼ pound **haricots verts** (thin green beans) or regular green beans, stem ends trimmed

¼ cup **pine nuts**

1 cup fresh **basil**, about 20 leaves

½ cup fresh **tarragon**, leaves stripped from 10 to 12 stems

    A handful of fresh **flat-leaf parsley**

    Zest of 1 lemon

1 **garlic clove**, peeled

½ cup grated **Parmigiano-Reggiano** cheese, a couple of handfuls, plus more to pass at the table

    Coarse black pepper

⅓ cup **EVOO** (extra-virgin olive oil; eyeball it)

Bring a large pot of water to a boil for the pasta. Salt the water, add the pasta, and cook to al dente; it should still have a bite to it. Cut the asparagus spears on an angle into 2-inch pieces. Cut the zucchini into matchsticks. Cut the haricots verts or green beans on an angle into 2-inch pieces. Add the vegetables to the pot with the pasta after the penne has been cooking for about 5 minutes. Boil the veggies and pasta together for 2 minutes.

While the pasta is working, toast the pine nuts in a small dry skillet until golden, then cool. Place the nuts, basil, tarragon, parsley, lemon zest, garlic, 1/2 cup of cheese, and a little salt and pepper in a food processor. Turn the processor on and stream in the EVOO until a thick sauce forms.

Scrape the pesto into a large, shallow serving dish. Add a ladle of hot, starchy pasta water to the pesto. Drain the penne and veggies and immediately add them to the pesto. Toss to coat the pasta and vegetables evenly. Adjust the salt and pepper to taste. Serve with extra grated cheese to pass at the table.

EXPRESS LANE
SHOPPING LIST

☐ 1/2 pound asparagus

☐ 1 small zucchini

☐ 1/4 pound (2 handfuls) haricots verts or green beans

☐ 1/4 cup pine nuts

☐ 1 bunch fresh basil

☐ 1 bunch fresh tarragon

And make sure you have the following On Hand:

Salt • Penne rigate • Flat-leaf parsley • Lemon • Garlic • Parmigiano-Reggiano cheese • Coarse black pepper • EVOO

Steak, Fried Onions, and Potatoes Salad Bowl with Blue Cheese Vinaigrette

This is like a steak dinner with onion rings, steak fries, and salad with blue cheese dressing, all chopped up in a bowl together. If you skipped lunch, this is your payoff.

4 SERVINGS

1⅓ pounds very thin cut **beef shell steak** (½ inch thick)

⅓ cup **EVOO** (extra-virgin olive oil), plus some for coating the meat

Grill seasoning, such as McCormick's Montreal Steak Seasoning

1 tablespoon **Worcestershire sauce** (eyeball it)

2 teaspoons **Dijon mustard**

3 tablespoons **red wine vinegar** (eyeball it)

⅓ pound **blue cheese**

Salt and **black pepper**

4 cups chopped **romaine**, 2 hearts

2 cups chopped **arugula** or watercress, 1 large bunch

½ cup canned **fried potato sticks**, a couple of handfuls

½ cup canned **fried onions**

❑ 1⅓ pounds very thin cut
beef shell steak

❑ ⅓ pound blue cheese

❑ 2 hearts romaine

❑ 1 large bunch arugula or
watercress

❑ 1 can fried potato sticks

❑ 1 can fried onions, such as
Durkee brand (they come
in those paper cans with
metal tops, like fried
potato sticks)

Preheat a large griddle or grill pan over high heat. Coat the meat with EVOO, then season on both sides with grill seasoning. Cook the meat for 3 minutes on each side, then let it rest for 10 minutes to cool a bit.

While the meat cooks, assemble the dressing: In a medium bowl, whisk together the Worcestershire, mustard, and red wine vinegar. Stream in about ⅓ cup EVOO while whisking constantly. Crumble the blue cheese into the bowl and stir it into the dressing. Season the dressing with salt and pepper.

Chop the rested steak into bite-size pieces. Place the chopped greens in a salad bowl and toss with the chopped steak, potato sticks, fried onions, and blue cheese dressing. Yum-o!

**And make sure you have
the following On Hand:**

EVOO • Grill seasoning •
Worcestershire • Dijon
mustard • Red wine vinegar
• Salt and black pepper

Turkey Burgers with Horseradish and Cheddar Cheese

I am the self-proclaimed "Queen of Burgers"—this is probably my 140th burger recipe! Ground meat is so versatile and accessible. Who *doesn't* love a good burger? This one combines lean ground turkey breast with spicy horseradish, sharp Cheddar, and tangy cranberry sauce. Yum-o!

4 SERVINGS

- 1 package **ground turkey breast**
- 2 rounded tablespoons **prepared horseradish**
- 1/3 pound sharp white **Cheddar cheese**, diced or crumbled into 1/4-inch pieces
- 2 **scallions**, finely chopped
- 1 rounded palmful **grill seasoning**, such as McCormick's Montreal Steak Seasoning

    EVOO (extra-virgin olive oil), for drizzling

    Spicy brown mustard

- 4 poppy seed **Kaiser rolls**, split
- 1 tub or can of good-quality **whole-berry cranberry sauce**

    Romaine lettuce leaves, for topping burgers

    Gourmet potato chips

Heat a nonstick skillet over medium-high heat.

In a medium bowl, mix together the meat, horseradish, Cheddar pieces, scallions, and grill seasoning. Form 4 patties and drizzle them with EVOO. Cook the burgers for 5 to 6 minutes on each side. Spread mustard on the bun bottoms and cranberry sauce on the bun tops. Place the burgers on the bun bottoms, top with romaine leaves, and set the bun tops in place. Serve fancy chips alongside.

EXPRESS LANE SHOPPING LIST

- ❑ 1 package ground turkey breast (1⅓ pounds is the average weight)
- ❑ 1 small jar prepared horseradish
- ❑ ⅓ pound sharp white Cheddar cheese
- ❑ 1 bunch scallions
- ❑ 4 poppy seed Kaiser rolls
- ❑ 1 tub or can of good-quality whole-berry cranberry sauce
- ❑ 1 head romaine lettuce
- ❑ 1 sack gourmet potato chips, any variety

And make sure you have the following On Hand:

Grill seasoning • EVOO • Spicy brown mustard

Which Came First? Chicken and Egg Sammies Deluxe

I dunno who came first, but I'm glad they met up in my sandwich! This simple sammy supper stacks together cutlets, egg, cheese, and greens, all in one bun. It's so good it's why the chicken crossed the road.

4 SERVINGS

1½ pounds **chicken breast cutlets**

2 teaspoons **smoked paprika**

   Salt and **black pepper**

4 tablespoons **EVOO** (extra-virgin olive oil)

4 large **eggs**

2 tablespoons **milk** or half-and-half, whichever you keep on hand for coffee

2 **jarred roasted red peppers**, patted dry and chopped

   A handful of fresh **flat-leaf parsley**, chopped

4 **crusty rolls**, split

4 slices **smoked Gouda** cheese

2 cups chopped **watercress** (from 1 bunch)

Preheat the broiler.

Season the chicken breast cutlets evenly with smoked paprika, salt, and pepper. Heat 2 tablespoons of the EVOO, twice around the pan, in a large nonstick skillet over medium-high heat. Add the chicken to the pan and cook for 2 to 3 minutes on each side. Remove the chicken from the skillet and let it rest, tented with foil. Wipe out the pan and add the remaining 2 tablespoons of EVOO. In a small bowl, beat the eggs with salt, pepper, and milk or half-and-half. Add the roasted peppers and parsley to the skillet and cook for 30 seconds, then add the eggs and scramble to your desired doneness with a wooden spoon or spatula.

While the eggs cook, toast the rolls under the broiler, 1 minute, then remove them to a work surface. Keep the broiler on.

To assemble, slice the chicken and pile it on the roll bottoms. Top each sammy with one quarter of the eggs and a slice of cheese. Place the sammies back under the broiler for 30 seconds to melt the cheese. Reserve the tops. When the cheese has melted, transfer the sammies to plates and top them with a pile of watercress, then set the roll tops in place.

EXPRESS LANE
SHOPPING LIST

❑ 1½ pounds chicken breast cutlets

❑ 4 crusty rolls

❑ 4 slices smoked Gouda cheese

❑ 1 bunch watercress

And make sure you have the following On Hand:

Smoked paprika • Salt and black pepper • EVOO • Eggs • Milk or half-and-half • Jarred roasted red peppers • Flat-leaf parsley

Pappa al Pomodoro

Pappa al Pomodoro is Tuscan stale bread soup. It is a favorite of my mom, Elsa. When we are both tired this is a good go-to recipe: pappa for my mama.

Use a vegetable peeler to curl off nice big shavings of Parmigiano-Reggiano to float on top of the soup.

4 SERVINGS

- 1 loaf **chewy bread**, such as ciabatta
- ½ cup **EVOO** (extra-virgin olive oil)
- 1 sprig fresh **rosemary**
- 4 **garlic cloves**, chopped
- 1 small **onion**
- 1 cup **chicken stock**
- 1 14-ounce can **diced tomatoes**
- 1 28-ounce can **crushed tomatoes**
- 1 cup fresh **basil**, about 20 leaves

   Salt and **black pepper**

   Freshly shaved **Parmigiano-Reggiano** or grated Pecorino Romano cheese

EXPRESS LANE
SHOPPING LIST

❑ 1 loaf chewy bread, such as
   ciabatta

❑ 1 bunch fresh **rosemary**

❑ 1 bunch fresh **basil**

Chop about 2 cups (a couple of small mounds) of the bread and reserve the rest to pass at the table.

Heat a medium soup pot over medium heat. Add about ¼ cup of the EVOO, 4 times around the pan, then add the sprig of rosemary and the garlic. Peel and halve the onion and, using a box grater or other hand-held grater, grate the onion directly into the soup pot. Sauté the mixture for 5 minutes, then remove the rosemary stem. Add the chicken stock and the tomatoes and bring it to a bubble. Add the bread chunks and stir until the bread has melted into the soup; the result is a soup-er thick consistency. Tear or shred the basil and stir it into the soup. Season the soup with salt and pepper to taste and ladle the soup into bowls. Top it with an extra swirl of EVOO, 1 tablespoon per bowl, and lots of shaved Parm or grated Pecorino Romano cheese.

And make sure you have the following On Hand:

EVOO • Garlic • Onion • Chicken stock • Canned diced tomatoes • Canned crushed tomatoes • Salt and black pepper • Parmigiano-Reggiano or Pecorino Romano cheese

Black Forest Reubens

When is a sammy not just a sammy? When it's a meal! Try wrapping your mouth around this riff on a Reuben.

4 SERVINGS

- 8 slices **pumpernickel bread**
- 4 tablespoons (½ stick) **butter**, softened
- 3 rounded tablespoonfuls **dill pickle relish**
- 1 **shallot**, finely chopped
- 1 rounded tablespoon **capers**, chopped
- 4 rounded tablespoonfuls **spicy brown mustard**
- 16 deli slices **Swiss cheese**, such as Emmentaler
- ¾ pound deli-sliced **corned beef**
- ¾ pound deli-sliced **Black Forest ham**
- 1 jar **cooked red cabbage** or 1 pouch sauerkraut
- 4 large **half-sour pickles** or garlic pickles
- **Gourmet potato chips**

Spread one side of each bread slice with softened butter. In a small bowl, mix together the relish, shallots, capers, and mustard. Build the sandwiches with buttered sides of the bread facing out: slather a liberal amount of the mustard mixture on 4 slices, then top with a slice of Swiss, one fourth of the corned beef, one fourth of the ham, a small mound of drained red cabbage or sauerkraut, another slice of cheese, and finally another slice of bread.

Heat a nonstick skillet over medium heat. Toast the Reubens for 5 to 6 minutes on each side until the cheese melts. Cut the sammies in half and serve with pickles and chips.

EXPRESS LANE SHOPPING LIST

- ❏ 1 loaf sliced pumpernickel bread
- ❏ 1 jar dill pickle relish
- ❏ ½ pound deli-sliced Swiss cheese, such as Emmentaler
- ❏ ¾ pound deli-sliced corned beef
- ❏ ¾ pound deli-sliced Black Forest ham
- ❏ 1 jar cooked red cabbage, available on the canned vegetable aisle, or 1 pouch sauerkraut
- ❏ 4 large half-sour pickles or garlic pickles from the deli counter
- ❏ 1 sack gourmet potato chips, any variety

And make sure you have the following On Hand:

Butter • Shallot • Capers • Spicy brown mustard

Spinach-Artichoke Cheesy Tortellini

If you like those spinach and artichoke dips you get on the appetizer menu in restaurants, you're gonna LOVE this!

4 SERVINGS

- 1 10-ounce box **frozen spinach**
- 2 tablespoons **EVOO** (extra-virgin olive oil), twice around the pan
- 1 tablespoon **butter**
- 3 **garlic cloves**, chopped
- 1 small **onion**, peeled and halved
- 2 tablespoons all-purpose **flour**
- 1 cup **chicken stock**
- 1 cup **heavy cream**
- ⅛ teaspoon freshly grated **nutmeg** (eyeball it)
- 1 14-ounce can **artichoke hearts** in water, drained and chopped

  A couple of handfuls grated **Parmigiano-Reggiano** or Pecorino Romano cheese

  Salt and **black pepper**
- 1 pound **cheese tortellini** or flavored tortellini, such as wild mushroom

EXPRESS LANE
SHOPPING LIST

❑ 1 14-ounce can artichoke
    hearts in water

❑ 1 pound cheese tortellini
    or flavored tortellini

Bring a large pot of water to a boil to cook the pasta. Microwave the spinach on high for 6 minutes to defrost.

Heat a deep skillet over medium heat with the EVOO and butter. When the butter melts and is hot, add the garlic. Using a box grater, grate the onion directly into the skillet. Sauté the onions and garlic for 5 minutes. Sprinkle the flour into the skillet and cook for 1 minute. Whisk in the stock, then the cream, and bring the sauce to a bubble. Season the sauce with nutmeg and reduce the heat to low.

Place the defrosted spinach in a clean kitchen towel and wring it dry. Separate it as you add it to the sauce. Stir in the chopped artichokes and a couple handfuls of cheese, then season the spinach-artichoke sauce with salt and pepper.

Salt the boiling water and cook the tortellini according to package directions, about 3 to 5 minutes. Drain it well and toss with the spinach-artichoke sauce. Serve immediately.

And make sure you have the following On Hand:

Frozen spinach • EVOO •
Butter • Garlic • Onion
• Flour • Chicken stock •
Heavy cream • Nutmeg •
Parmigiano-Reggiano or
Pecorino Romano cheese
• Salt and black pepper

Warm Chopped Chicken Piccata Spinach Salad

Love Chicken Piccata? Try this warm and flavorful super-salad-supper!

4 SERVINGS

- 6 **chicken breast cutlets**
- **Salt** and **black pepper**
- 3 tablespoons **EVOO** (extra-virgin olive oil)
- 4 chewy, **crusty rolls**
- 1 tablespoon **butter**
- 2 **shallots**, chopped
- 3 **garlic cloves**, chopped
- 3 tablespoons **capers**, chopped
- ½ cup **dry white wine**
- **Juice of 1 lemon**
- 2 pounds triple-washed **spinach**, tough stems removed, coarsely chopped
- **Parmigiano-Reggiano** cheese, for garnish

Preheat the oven to 250°F.

Season the chicken with salt and pepper on both sides. Heat your largest nonstick skillet with 2 tablespoons of the EVOO, twice around the pan, over medium-high heat. When the oil ripples, add the chicken and cook for 3 minutes on each side. Remove the chicken to a plate and let it rest and cool.

Wrap the rolls in foil and place in the oven to warm.

To the same skillet, add the remaining tablespoon of EVOO, once around the pan, and the butter. Melt the butter into the EVOO and add the shallots, garlic, and capers. Sauté for 5 minutes, then add the white wine and reduce for 30 seconds. Next, add the lemon juice and immediately add the spinach—mound it up in the pan. You will not be able to fit it all in there at first; just keep turning the spinach and wilting it down until you get it all in, then turn the heat off. Keep some leaves a bit crisp to vary the textures in your salad. Season the spinach with salt and pepper. Chop the chicken into little bits, then add to the warm salad and toss to distribute. Divide the salad among the plates and garnish it with shaved Parmigiano-Reggiano. Serve with a warm roll for mopping.

EXPRESS LANE
SHOPPING LIST

❑ 6 chicken breast cutlets, about 1 pound

❑ 4 chewy, crusty rolls

❑ 2 pounds triple-washed spinach

And make sure you have the following On Hand:

Salt and black pepper •
EVOO • Butter • Shallots •
Garlic • Capers • Dry white
wine • Lemon •
Parmigiano-Reggiano cheese

Toasted Garlic and Sweet Pea Pasta

Nutty toasted garlic and sweet peas? Oh, my! I could eat the whole potful myself, then drift off into sweet dreams!

4 SERVINGS

      Salt

1   pound **long-cut pasta**, whatever you have in the cupboard

¼ to ⅓ cup **EVOO** (extra-virgin olive oil; eyeball it)

5   large **garlic cloves**, very thinly sliced *GoodFellas* style (Just do your best. No one can top Paulie!)

¼ teaspoon **red pepper flakes** (eyeball it)

1   large **onion**, finely chopped

½ teaspoon **dried thyme** (eyeball it)

      Black pepper

¾ cup **white wine** (eyeball it)

2   cups **chicken stock**

2   10-ounce boxes **frozen peas**

½ cup fresh **flat-leaf parsley**, a couple of generous handfuls, chopped

1   cup grated **Parmigiano-Reggiano** or Pecorino Romano cheese, plus some to pass at the table

And make sure you have
the following On Hand:

Salt • Long-cut pasta •
EVOO • Garlic • Red pepper
flakes • Onion • Dried thyme
• Black pepper • White wine
• Chicken stock • Frozen
peas • Flat-leaf parsley •
Parmigiano-Reggiano or
Pecorino Romano cheese

Place a large pot of water with a tight-fitting lid over high heat and bring it to a boil to cook the pasta. Once it comes up to a boil, add salt and the pasta. Cook according to package directions until al dente. Heads up: right before draining you will need to reserve about ½ cup of the starchy cooking liquid.

While the water is coming up to a boil, add the EVOO, 4 healthy times around the pan, and the sliced garlic to a large skillet. Place the skillet over medium heat, spread the sliced garlic out in an even layer in the heating oil, and keep an eye on the garlic—it can go from golden to burnt in a couple of seconds. Have a slotted spoon and some paper towels on a plate nearby. Once the garlic is toasty brown, remove it from the oil with the slotted spoon and drain it on the paper towels.

Turn the heat up under the EVOO to medium high, then add the red pepper flakes, onions, thyme, salt, and a little pepper. Cook, stirring frequently, for about 5 minutes or until the onions become tender and lightly browned. Add the wine and cook for 2 minutes, then add the chicken stock and continue to cook for another 2 minutes. Add the peas and a couple of ladles of the pasta cooking liquid. Bring the sauce back to a bubble. With the back of a spoon mash about half of the peas in the skillet. Add the parsley and toasted garlic slices, stir to combine, then give it a taste and add more salt and pepper if you think it needs it. Add the cooked drained pasta and toss to coat in the sauce. If the sauce is too thick, add another glug of chicken stock. Stir in the cheese, then transfer the pasta to serving plates. Pass extra cheese at the table.

Smoky Sweet-Potato Chicken Stoup

This stoup will quickly become one of your comfort food favorites, promise!

4 SERVINGS

2 tablespoons **EVOO** (extra-virgin olive oil), twice around the pan

2 medium **carrots**, peeled

2 **celery ribs**

1 large **onion**, peeled and halved

1 large **sweet potato**

2 **garlic cloves**, chopped

1 **chipotle chili in adobo**, finely chopped

Salt and black pepper

½ teaspoon **dried thyme** (eyeball it)

1 **bay leaf**

1 cup **dry white wine** (eyeball it)

1 quart plus 1 cup **chicken stock**

1 package **chicken tenders**, cut into bite-size pieces

4 **scallions**, thinly sliced

¼ cup fresh **cilantro leaves**, a generous handful, coarsely chopped

½ cup **sour cream**, for garnish (optional)

Heat a soup pot over medium-high heat with the EVOO. While the oil heats, cut the carrots in half lengthwise, then slice into thin half moons. Add the carrots to the pot, stirring to coat the carrots in the oil. Chop and drop in the celery and onion, chopping them as small as you can, but don't make yourself crazy.

Peel and then cut the sweet potato into quarters lengthwise, then thinly slice them into bite-size pieces. Add the sweet potatoes, garlic, and chipotle and stir to combine. Season the veggies with salt and pepper, the thyme, and the bay leaf. Cook the veggies together for 1 minute. Add the wine to the vegetables and reduce for a minute. Add the stock to the pot, cover the pot, and raise the heat to high.

When the stoup boils, remove the cover and simmer over low heat for 10 minutes. Add the cut-up chicken and simmer for 5 minutes, or until the sweet potatoes are tender and the chicken is cooked through. Turn the heat off, discard the bay leaf, and stir in the scallions and cilantro. Serve each portion of stoup with a dollop of sour cream on top.

EXPRESS LANE SHOPPING LIST

- ❑ **1 large** sweet potato
- ❑ **1 package** chicken tenders (about ¾ **to 1 pound**)
- ❑ **1 bunch** scallions
- ❑ **1 bunch fresh** cilantro
- ❑ **Small container** sour cream **(optional)**

And make sure you have the following On Hand:

EVOO • Carrots • Celery • Onion • Garlic • Canned chipotle chili in adobo • Salt and black pepper • Dried thyme • Bay leaf • Dry white wine • Chicken stock

Chorizo-Cod-Potato Stew

I know, I know, you're exhausted. Well, let me tell you, this stew is easy to make, is good for you, and has a big satisfying flavor. You'll be slurping away in front of the TV before you know it . . . and then you can go to bed, early, like your mom always said you should.

4 SERVINGS

- 2 tablespoons **EVOO** (extra-virgin olive oil), twice around the pan
- ½ pound **chorizo** or andouille sausage, thinly sliced
- 5 red or white **boiling potatoes**, cut in half, then thinly sliced into half moons
- 1 large **onion**, chopped
- 1 **carrot**, peeled, cut in half lengthwise, and sliced into half moons
- 4 **garlic cloves**, chopped

  Salt and black pepper
- 1 cup **dry white wine** (eyeball it)
- 1 14-ounce can diced **fire-roasted tomatoes**
- 1 quart **chicken stock**
- 2 **jarred roasted red peppers**, chopped
- 1½ pounds **fresh cod**, cut into 2-inch chunks
- ½ cup fresh **flat-leaf parsley**, a couple of generous handfuls, chopped

Preheat a soup pot over medium-high heat with the EVOO. Add the sliced chorizo and cook, stirring frequently, for 2 minutes. Add the potatoes and continue to cook for 2 minutes. Add the onions, carrots, and garlic, season with salt and pepper, and cook, stirring frequently, for 5 minutes. Add the white wine and cook for 3 minutes. Add the fire-roasted tomatoes, chicken stock, and roasted red peppers, bring up to a simmer and cook for 5 minutes. You want the soup to be at a gentle simmer before you add the fish so, if necessary, turn the heat down a little. Add the cod. Gently simmer for 3 to 4 minutes, or until the fish is cooked through. Finish the soup with the parsley, taste for seasoning, and serve.

Open-Face Blue Moon Burgers with 'Shrooms

Here's another one of my Better Burgers. This one comes out looking so impressive I would serve it even when I entertain (were I not so exhausted!).

4 SERVINGS

- 2 pounds **ground sirloin**
- 1 tablespoon **Worcestershire sauce** (eyeball it)
- 1 **shallot**, finely chopped

  Salt and **black pepper**
- 2 tablespoons **EVOO** (extra-virgin olive oil), plus some for drizzling
- 2 tablespoons **butter**
- ½ pound **button mushrooms**, trimmed and thinly sliced
- ½ pound **cremini mushrooms**, trimmed and thinly sliced
- ½ small **onion**, finely chopped
- 2 large **garlic cloves**, chopped
- ½ cup **chicken stock**
- ¼ cup fresh **flat-leaf parsley**, chopped, a generous handful
- 4 thick slices country-style **crusty bread**
- 10 fresh **basil leaves**, about ½ cup
- 1 small bunch **arugula**, washed and thick stems removed
- 1 **red beefsteak tomato**, cut into 4 thick slices
- 1 **yellow beefsteak tomato**, cut into 4 thick slices
- 4 ounces good-quality **blue cheese**, crumbled

In a mixing bowl, combine the ground sirloin, Worcestershire sauce, and chopped shallot. Mix thoroughly. Score the meat with your hand, marking 4 equal portions. Form each portion into a large 1-inch-thick patty. Preheat a nonstick skillet over medium-high heat. Season the patties liberally with some salt and pepper and then drizzle the patties with a little EVOO and place in the hot skillet. Cook for 5 to 6 minutes per side, or until the patties are firm to the touch and cooked through.

Preheat the broiler.

While the burgers are cooking, preheat a second large skillet over medium-high heat with the 2 tablespoons of EVOO, twice around the pan, and the butter. Add the mushrooms to the skillet and spread them out in an even layer, resisting the temptation to stir for a few minutes to let the mushrooms start to brown. Once brown, go ahead and stir, continuing to cook for 2 minutes, then add the onions and garlic and season with salt and pepper. Continue to cook, stirring every now and then, for about 3 minutes, or until the onions start to look tender. Add the chicken stock, bring it up to a bubble, and simmer for about 2 minutes. Add the parsley and stir to combine; taste and adjust the seasoning with salt and pepper.

While the burgers and the mushrooms are working, toast the bread slices under the broiler until they are golden on both sides.

Coarsely chop the basil and arugula.

Place a piece of toast on each serving plate. Top each piece of toast with 1 slice of red tomato and 1 slice of yellow tomato and season the tomatoes with a little salt and pepper. Sprinkle the tomatoes with the arugula-basil mixture and put a cooked burger on top of that. Add the blue cheese crumbles to the mushrooms, stir to combine, and top each burger with the mushroom–blue cheese mixture. Grab a fork and a knife and dig in.

EXPRESS LANE SHOPPING LIST

- ❏ **2 pounds** ground sirloin
- ❏ **½ pound** button mushrooms
- ❏ **½ pound** cremini mushrooms
- ❏ **1 loaf** country-style crusty bread
- ❏ **1 bunch** fresh basil
- ❏ **1 small bunch** arugula
- ❏ **1 red** beefsteak tomato
- ❏ **1 yellow** beefsteak tomato (if yellow is not available get another red one)
- ❏ **4 ounces** good-quality blue cheese

And make sure you have the following On Hand:

Worcestershire • Shallot • Salt and black pepper • EVOO • Butter • Onion • Garlic • Chicken stock • Flat-leaf parsley

Cowboy Spaghetti

Eat this meal in front of the TV. Invite Clint Eastwood and the cast of your favorite spaghetti western (mine's *The Good, the Bad, and the Ugly*).

4 SERVINGS

Salt

1 pound **spaghetti**

1 tablespoon **EVOO** (extra-virgin olive oil), once around the pan

3 slices **smoky bacon**, chopped

1 pound **ground sirloin**

1 medium **onion**

3 to 4 **garlic cloves**, chopped

Black pepper

2 teaspoons **hot sauce** (eyeball it)

1 tablespoon **Worcestershire sauce** (eyeball it)

1 14-ounce can chopped or crushed **fire-roasted tomatoes**

1 8-ounce can **tomato sauce**

8 ounces sharp **Cheddar** cheese

4 **scallions**, trimmed, chopped

Bring a large pot of water to a boil. Salt the water and add the spaghetti. Cook the pasta to al dente, with a bite to it. Drain the spaghetti.

Heat a deep skillet over medium-high heat. Add the EVOO and bacon. Brown and crisp the bacon for 5 minutes, then remove with a slotted spoon to a paper-towel-lined plate. Drain off a little excess fat from the skillet if necessary, leaving just enough to coat the bottom. Add the beef and crumble it as it browns, 3 to 4 minutes. Add the onions and garlic and stir into the meat. Season the meat with salt and pepper, hot sauce, and Worcestershire. Cook for 5 to 6 minutes more, then stir in the tomatoes and tomato sauce.

Add the hot spaghetti to the meat and sauce and combine. Adjust the seasonings and serve up the pasta in shallow bowls. Grate some cheese over the pasta and sprinkle with the scallions.

EXPRESS LANE
SHOPPING LIST

❑ 1 pound ground sirloin
❑ 8 ounces sharp Cheddar cheese
❑ 1 bunch scallions

And make sure you have the following On Hand:

Salt • Spaghetti • EVOO • Smoky bacon • Onion • Garlic • Black pepper • Hot sauce • Worcestershire • Canned chopped or crushed fire-roasted tomatoes • Canned tomato sauce

Seared Tuna Steaks on White Beans with Grape Tomatoes and Garlic Chips

Meaty, easy, and Mediterranean-style, this recipe will make any list of favorites.

4 SERVINGS

- 4 tablespoons **EVOO** (extra-virgin olive oil), plus some for drizzling
- 5 large **garlic cloves**, very thinly sliced—just do your best
- 1 large **onion**, sliced
- 3 **celery ribs**, finely chopped
- 1 large pinch **red pepper flakes**
  Salt and **black pepper**
- 4 6-ounce **tuna steaks**, about 1½ inches thick
- ¾ cup **white wine**, a few good glugs
- 1¼ cups **chicken stock**
- 2 14-ounce cans **cannellini beans**, rinsed and drained
- 1 pint **grape tomatoes**
- ½ cup fresh **flat-leaf parsley**, a couple of generous handfuls, chopped
  Juice of ½ lemon

Place a medium-size skillet on the stovetop with the 4 tablespoons of EVOO, 4 times around the pan. Add the sliced garlic and spread it out in one layer in the oil. Turn the heat on to medium low to slowly brown the garlic, about 2 to 3 minutes. With a slotted spoon, remove the garlic chips to a paper-towel-lined plate, leaving the oil in the skillet. Turn the heat up to medium high; add the onions, celery, red pepper flakes, salt, and pepper. Cook for 5 minutes, until the onions take on a little color and become nice and tender.

While the onions are browning, place a large nonstick skillet over high heat. Pat the tuna steaks dry and drizzle with a little EVOO, coating the steaks evenly. Season the steaks with salt and pepper. When the pan is very hot, add the tuna steaks. Sear and brown the steaks on one side for 2 minutes, then turn and immediately reduce the heat to medium. Loosely cover the pan with an aluminum foil tent and cook the steaks 5 minutes for rare, 7 minutes for medium. The steaks should be firm but have a little give, and some pink should remain at the center.

While the tuna is cooking, add the white wine and chicken stock to the onions and celery. Bring up to a bubble and continue to cook for about 3 minutes. Add the white beans and grape tomatoes and continue to cook until the beans and tomatoes are warmed through, about 2 minutes. Finish the beans with the parsley, garlic chips, and lemon juice and stir to distribute.

To serve, pile a serving of beans on each dinner plate and top with a tuna steak.

Smoky Black Bean and Rice Stoup

This is a chop, drop, and open recipe. Place your cutting board next to the stove, heat up the pots, chop everything on the board, drop it into the pan, then open up your cans. As soon as the stoup bubbles, dinner is done.

4 SERVINGS

- 2 tablespoons **EVOO** (extra-virgin olive oil), twice around the pan
- 3 **bacon slices**, chopped
- 1 **bay leaf**
- 2 **celery ribs**, chopped
- 1 medium **onion**, chopped
- 4 **garlic cloves**, chopped
- 1 cup **frozen corn kernels**
- 2 15-ounce cans **black beans**
- 1 tablespoon **ground coriander**, a palmful
- 1 tablespoon **chili powder**, a palmful
- 1½ teaspoons **ground cumin**, ½ palmful
- 1 tablespoon **Worcestershire sauce** (eyeball it)
- 2 teaspoons **hot sauce** (eyeball it)
  Coarse salt and **coarse black pepper**
- 1 15-ounce can diced **fire-roasted tomatoes**, such as Muir Glen
- 1 8-ounce can **tomato sauce**
- 1 quart **chicken stock**
- 1 cup **white rice**

Heat a medium soup pot over medium-high heat. Add the EVOO, then add the bacon and cook for 3 to 4 minutes to render the fat. Add the bay leaf, celery, onions, and garlic and cook for 3 to 4 minutes to soften the veggies. Add the corn and 1 can of black beans and their juice. Drain the other can, then add half the can of beans. Mash the remaining beans in the can with a fork to make a paste out of them, then scrape them into the soup pot—this will make the stoup souper-thick! Season the veggies and beans with the coriander, chili, ground cumin, Worcestershire, and hot sauce. Season the mixture with salt and pepper to taste. Stir in the tomatoes, tomato sauce, and stock, then cover the pot and raise the heat to bring the stoup to a boil. Add the rice and cook the stoup over a rolling simmer until the rice is tender but has a little bite left to it, 15 minutes. Adjust the seasonings and serve.

Hungry-Man Bloody-Mary Burgers and Spicy Garlic-Roasted Broccoli

A friend recommended that I add a little fresh dill and lime juice to my regular Bloody Mary concoction. I gave it a shot and it was great! The dill and lime punched up all the flavors without taking them over. I've applied that trick to these burgers.

4 SERVINGS

¼ cup **EVOO** (extra-virgin olive oil), plus some for drizzling

4 to 5 **garlic cloves**, finely chopped

1 tablespoon **chili powder**, a palmful

Salt and **black pepper**

1 large head **broccoli**, cut into thin, long spears

2 **celery ribs**, finely chopped

½ pint **grape tomatoes**, halved

3 to 4 sprigs **fresh dill**, chopped

¼ cup fresh **flat-leaf parsley**, a generous handful, chopped

Juice of 1 lime

3 tablespoons **mayonnaise**

2 pounds **ground sirloin**

2 tablespoons **prepared horseradish**

1½ teaspoons **celery salt**, half a palmful

2 tablespoons **Worcestershire sauce** (eyeball it)

2 teaspoons **hot sauce** (eyeball it)

4 sandwich-size **English muffins**

Preheat the oven to 425°F.

Place the ¼ cup of EVOO, the garlic, chili powder, and a little salt and pepper in the bottom of a large bowl and add the broccoli spears. Toss to coat the broccoli evenly, then transfer to a large nonstick baking sheet. Roast the broccoli until the ends are crisp and brown and the stalks are tender, 17 to 20 minutes.

To make the burger topping, in a bowl combine the chopped celery and the grape tomato halves with the dill, parsley, lime juice, and mayonnaise. Use the back of a fork to smash up the tomatoes while you incorporate them into the sauce.

In a mixing bowl, combine the ground sirloin, horseradish, celery salt, Worcestershire sauce, hot sauce, and a little pepper. Mix thoroughly. Score the meat with your hand marking 4 equal portions. Form each portion into a large, 1-inch-thick patty. Preheat a nonstick skillet over medium-high heat. Drizzle EVOO over the patties and place them into the hot skillet. Cook for 5 to 6 minutes per side, until the patties become firm to the touch and are cooked through.

While the burgers are cooking, toast the English muffins. Remove the burgers to the bottoms of the toasted English muffins, add some of the celery-tomato topping, and then cover with the muffin tops. Serve the spicy garlic broccoli alongside.

Chicken with Scallion-Lime Sauce and Sweet Carrot Rice

Sweet and simply delicious, this dish is a real mild-child, for nights when you feel less than wild.

4 SERVINGS

        4 tablespoons **EVOO** (extra-virgin olive oil)
        3 large **carrots**, peeled and grated
           Salt and **black pepper**
    1½ cups **white rice**
        3 cups **chicken stock**
        1 teaspoon **dried thyme**, ⅓ palmful
           Zest and juice of 2 limes
        4 boneless, **skinless chicken breasts**
        3 large **garlic cloves**, chopped
     ½ teaspoon **red pepper flakes** (eyeball it)
        1 teaspoon ground **coriander**, ⅓ palmful
        3 bunches of **scallions**, about 15, roots trimmed, sliced
     ¼ cup fresh **flat-leaf parsley**, a generous handful, chopped
        2 tablespoons **butter**

EXPRESS LANE
SHOPPING LIST

❑ **4 boneless**, skinless
chicken breasts,
6 ounces each

❑ **3 bunches of** scallions

Heat a medium pot with a tight-fitting lid over medium-high heat. Add about 1 tablespoon of the EVOO, once around the pan. Add the grated carrots and a little salt and pepper and cook, stirring, for 1 minute. Add the rice and stir to coat in the oil and distribute the carrots. Add 2½ cups of the chicken stock. Bring the stock to a boil, cover the pot, and reduce the heat to a simmer. Cook for 15 to 18 minutes, until the rice is tender.

Preheat a large skillet over medium-high heat. While the pan is heating up, combine 2 tablespoons of the EVOO, the thyme, lime zest, salt, and pepper in a shallow dish. Add the chicken breasts and coat thoroughly in the mixture. Add the seasoned chicken to the skillet and cook for 5 to 6 minutes on each side, or until cooked through. Transfer the chicken to a plate and cover it loosely with aluminum foil. Return the skillet to the heat; add the remaining tablespoon of EVOO. Add the garlic, red pepper flakes, and coriander. Cook, stirring constantly, for about 1 minute, then add the scallions and cook for 1 minute, again stirring constantly. Add the lime juice and the remaining ½ cup of chicken stock and continue to cook for about 2 minutes. Turn the heat off and add the parsley and butter, stirring and shaking the pan until the butter is completely melted.

To serve, slice the chicken on a slight angle. Divide the rice among 4 serving plates and top each pile of rice with a sliced chicken breast. Pour some scallion-lime sauce over each chicken breast.

And make sure you have the following On Hand:

EVOO • Carrots • Salt and black pepper • White rice • Chicken stock • Dried thyme • Limes • Garlic • Red pepper flakes • Ground coriander • Flat-leaf parsley • Butter

Pasta in a Creamy Artichoke and Saffron Sauce

The saffron does all the work for you in this dish—you'll freak out when you take your first bite and actually *taste* how easy this was to make. Since you now have saffron on hand, next time you're making regular old rice, add a pinch of saffron and your rice will taste extraordinary.

4 SERVINGS

Salt

1 pound long-cut or short-cut **pasta**

2 tablespoons **EVOO** (extra-virgin olive oil), plus some for drizzling

1 large **onion**, chopped

3 large **garlic cloves**, chopped

1 generous pinch **saffron**

Black pepper

¾ cup **white wine** (eyeball it)

1¼ cups **chicken stock**

About ⅓ cup **heavy cream** or half-and-half (eyeball it)

1 14-ounce can **artichoke hearts in water**, drained and thinly sliced

½ cup fresh **flat-leaf parsley**, a couple of generous handfuls, chopped

½ cup grated **Parmigiano-Reggiano** or Pecorino Romano cheese, plus some to pass at the table

6 cups **chopped greens**, romaine or mixed

Balsamic vinegar, for drizzling

Crusty bread

Place a large pot of water with a tight-fitting lid over high heat and bring it to a boil to cook the pasta. Once it comes up to a boil, add some salt and the pasta. Cook according to the package directions until al dente. Drain well.

While the pasta is cooking, preheat a large skillet over medium-high heat with the 2 tablespoons of EVOO, twice around the pan. Add the onions, garlic, saffron, salt, and pepper. Cook, stirring frequently, for about 4 minutes, or until the onions start to look tender. The onions will turn an outrageous yellow color, which is the saffron at work. Add the white wine; continue to cook until the wine has almost evaporated, about 3 minutes. Add the chicken stock and cream, then bring the sauce up to a bubble and simmer for about 4 minutes. Add the artichokes and cook until heated through, about 1 minute more. The sauce will be a beautiful yellow and will seem a little thin. Add the parsley and drained pasta and stir to combine with the sauce. The pasta will start soaking up the sauce right away. Turn the heat off, add the grated cheese, and stir to distribute. Taste and season the pasta with more salt and pepper to taste. Serve with a little extra grated cheese.

Drizzle the greens with balsamic vinegar and EVOO, season with some salt and pepper, and toss. Serve the salad alongside the pasta with the crusty bread.

Chicken with a Sweet Corn and Potato Sauté

I loved corn so much as a kid that you couldn't get that cob out of my hand for hours. In the summer months substitute fresh kernels scraped from the cob for the frozen.

4 SERVINGS

- 4 boneless, skinless chicken breasts
  Salt and black pepper
  Zest and juice of 1 lemon
- 2 large baking potatoes, scrubbed clean or peeled, it's up to you
- 4 tablespoons EVOO (extra-virgin olive oil)
- 1 teaspoon dried thyme, 1/3 palmful
- 1 medium onion, finely chopped
- 2 large garlic cloves, chopped
- 1 10-ounce box frozen corn kernels
- 1¼ cups chicken stock
- 2 tablespoons butter
- ¼ cup fresh flat-leaf parsley, a generous handful, chopped

Season the chicken breasts with salt, pepper, and the lemon juice. Let the chicken marinate while you get the rest of the meal going.

Cut the potatoes into quarters lengthwise. Arrange the quarters cut side down on a cutting board. Thinly slice the potatoes across the width—you want thin, bite-size pieces.

Heat a nonstick large skillet over medium-high heat with about 2 tablespoons of the EVOO, twice around the pan. Add the potatoes in an even layer across the hot skillet. Season the sliced spuds with salt, pepper, and the thyme. Resist the temptation to stir the potatoes for about 2 minutes, to let them brown up a little bit. Once the potatoes brown, stir in the onions and garlic and continue to cook, stirring occasionally, for 7 to 8 minutes, or until the potatoes are flirting with tenderness. If the potatoes are getting too dark, turn the heat back a little.

While the onions and potatoes are cooking, preheat a second large skillet with the remaining 2 tablespoons of EVOO. Add the chicken breasts and cook for 5 to 6 minutes on each side.

While the chicken is cooking, add the corn kernels to the potatoes and cook, stirring frequently, for 2 to 3 minutes. Add the chicken stock, turn the heat up to high, and bring the stock up to a bubble and continue to cook for 3 minutes, or until the liquids have reduced by half. Turn the heat off and add the butter, parsley, and lemon zest, stirring until the butter is completely melted.

Serve the chicken whole or sliced on top of the sweet corn and potato sauté.

And make sure you have the following On Hand:

Salt and black pepper • Lemon • Baking potatoes • EVOO • Dried thyme • Onion • Garlic • Frozen corn kernels • Chicken stock • Butter • Flat-leaf parsley

Chicken, Chorizo, and Hominy Stoup

Stoup is good food. Homemade? Well, that's even better.

4 SERVINGS

- 2 tablespoons **EVOO** (extra-virgin olive oil), twice around the pan
- ½ pound **chorizo** or andouille sausage, casings removed, cut in half lengthwise and then thinly sliced into half moons
- 1 teaspoon **ground cumin**, ⅓ palmful
- 1 teaspoon **ground coriander**, ⅓ palmful
- 1 **bay leaf**
- 1 large **onion**, chopped
- 3 large **garlic cloves**, chopped
- 3 **celery ribs**, chopped
- 1 **chipotle chili in adobo**, finely chopped

  Salt and **black pepper**
- ½ bunch **kale**, washed and trimmed of thick stems, leaves coarsely chopped
- 1 15-ounce can **hominy**
- 1 quart **chicken stock**
- 1½ to 2 pounds **chicken tenders**, cut into bite-size pieces

Preheat a soup pot over medium-high heat with the EVOO. Add the chorizo and cook for about 2 minutes. Add the cumin, coriander, bay leaf, onions, garlic, celery, chipotle, salt, and pepper and cook for about 5 minutes, stirring frequently. Add the kale, pushing it down into the pan to make it fit, then add the hominy and chicken stock and bring up to a bubble. Simmer for about 10 minutes. Add the chicken pieces and simmer for 5 minutes, or until cooked through. Remove the bay leaf and serve the stoup.

EXPRESS LANE SHOPPING LIST

- ❏ ½ pound chorizo or andouille sausage

- ❏ 1 bunch kale (you'll use half the bunch; chop and sauté the rest with garlic another night)

- ❏ 1 15-ounce can hominy (giant hulled corn kernels, found on the Mexican food aisle)

- ❏ 1½ to 2 pounds chicken tenders

And make sure you have the following On Hand:

EVOO • Ground cumin • Ground coriander • Bay leaf • Onion • Garlic • Celery • Canned chipotle chili in adobo • Salt and black pepper • Chicken stock

Pasta with Bacon, Tomatoes, and Cheese

The ingredients list is the whole sales pitch. Need I say more?

4 SERVINGS

Salt

1 pound **short-cut pasta**

1 tablespoon **EVOO** (extra-virgin olive oil), once around the pan, plus more for the greens

4 **bacon** slices, chopped

1 large **onion**, chopped

4 large **garlic cloves**, chopped

¼ teaspoon **red pepper flakes** (eyeball it)

Black pepper

½ cup **white wine**, a couple of good glugs

½ cup **chicken stock**

1 pint **grape tomatoes**

1 ball **fresh mozzarella**, cut into ¼-inch dice

1 bunch fresh **chives**, chopped

15 fresh **basil leaves**, chopped or torn, about ¾ cup

½ cup grated **Parmigiano-Reggiano** or Pecorino Romano cheese, plus some to pass at the table

6 cups **mixed greens**

Vinegar for the greens

Place a large pot of water with a tight-fitting lid over high heat and bring to a boil. Once it comes to a boil, add some salt and the pasta. Cook according to the package directions until al dente. Heads up: you need to reserve ½ cup of the cooking liquid before you drain the pasta.

While the pasta is cooking, start the sauce. Preheat a large skillet over medium-high heat; add the EVOO. Add the chopped bacon and cook, stirring every now and then, until crispy, about 2 to 3 minutes. Add the onions, garlic, red pepper flakes, and a little salt and pepper. Cook, stirring frequently, for about 5 minutes, or until the onions start to brown. Add the white wine and cook for 1 minute. Add the chicken stock and reserved pasta cooking liquid, then bring up to a bubble and simmer for 2 minutes. Add the grape tomatoes and cook them for about 30 seconds, just to start getting them hot and ready to burst. Add the cooked drained pasta, toss to coat in the sauce, and let some of the sauce soak in, about 1 minute. Turn the heat off and add the diced mozzarella, the chives, basil, grated cheese, and black pepper to taste. Dress the greens with oil and vinegar and serve with the pasta.

Balsamic Chicken with White Beans and Wilted Spinach

Another easy chicken dinner: good for you, a good go-to, and good to go!

4 SERVINGS

2 tablespoons **balsamic vinegar** (eyeball it)

4 tablespoons **EVOO** (extra-virgin olive oil)

1 tablespoon **grill seasoning** such as McCormick's Montreal Steak Seasoning, a palmful

4 boneless, skinless **chicken breasts**

2 medium **onions**, thinly sliced

4 large **garlic cloves**, chopped

1 teaspoon **dried thyme**, 1/3 palmful

1/4 teaspoon **red pepper flakes** (eyeball it)

Salt and **black pepper**

1 **bay leaf**

3/4 cup **white wine** (eyeball it)

2 cups **chicken stock**

1 14-ounce can **cannellini beans**, drained

1 12-ounce sack **baby spinach** or 3/4 pound from bulk bins, washed and patted dry

1/2 cup fresh **flat-leaf parsley**, a couple of generous handfuls, chopped

Juice of 1 lemon

EXPRESS LANE
SHOPPING LIST

❏ **4 boneless, skinless
chicken breasts,
6 ounces each**

❏ **1 12-ounce sack** baby
spinach **or ¾ pound** from
bulk bins

In a shallow dish, combine the balsamic vinegar, about 2 tablespoons of the EVOO, and the grill seasoning. Coat the chicken breasts in the mixture and set aside to marinate while you start the white beans and wilted spinach.

Heat a large skillet over medium-high heat with the remaining 2 tablespoons of EVOO, twice around the pan. Add the onions, garlic, thyme, red pepper flakes, salt, pepper, and bay leaf. Cook, stirring frequently, until the onions are a little brown, 3 to 4 minutes. Add the white wine and chicken stock, bring up to a bubble, and cook for 5 minutes.

Heat another large skillet over medium-high heat. When it is hot, add the chicken breasts and cook for 5 to 6 minutes on each side. Remove the chicken to a plate, cover loosely with foil, and let rest a few minutes.

Add the cannellini beans to the skillet with the onions and stir to combine. Cook for about 2 minutes or until the beans are heated through. Turn off the heat and discard the bay leaf. Stir in the spinach, parsley, and lemon juice. Toss and stir until the spinach wilts.

To serve, place a portion of the white beans and wilted spinach on each serving plate. Thickly slice each chicken breast on an angle and arrange over the beans and spinach.

**And make sure you have
the following On Hand:**

Balsamic vinegar • EVOO •
Grill seasoning • Onions •
Garlic • Dried thyme • Red
pepper flakes • Salt and
black pepper • Bay leaf •
White wine • Chicken stock
• Canned cannellini beans •
Flat-leaf parsley • Lemon

Pasta with Broccoli and Sausage with a Ricotta Surprise

Pasta with butter, ricotta, and Parm cheese is an Italian children's standard. Add a little broccoli—we grown-ups need our fiber—then be a kid again and enjoy.

4 SERVINGS

Salt

1 pound **short-cut pasta**, such as penne

1 cup **ricotta cheese**

Zest and juice of 1 lemon

Freshly ground **black pepper**

1 tablespoon **EVOO** (extra-virgin olive oil), once around the pan

1 pound **bulk sweet Italian sausage**

1 large head **broccoli**

1 medium **onion**, chopped

4 large **garlic cloves**, chopped

¼ teaspoon **red pepper flakes** (eyeball it)

1½ cups **chicken stock**

½ cup fresh **flat-leaf parsley**, a couple of generous handfuls, chopped

½ cup grated **Parmigiano-Reggiano** or Pecorino Romano cheese, plus some to pass at the table

Place a large pot of water with a tight-fitting lid over high heat and bring to a boil. Once it comes to a boil, add some salt and the pasta. Cook according to package directions until al dente. Heads up: you will need to use about ½ cup of the starchy cooking liquid for the sauce before you drain the pasta.

In a small mixing bowl, combine the ricotta cheese, lemon zest, salt, and a lot of freshly ground black pepper. Reserve the ricotta mixture on the countertop and let it come to room temp. The flavors of the cheese and lemon will develop as the cheese warms up.

Preheat a large skillet over medium-high heat with the EVOO. Add the sausage and break it up with the back of a wooden spoon into small bite-size pieces. Really go at breaking the meat up; it will make a big difference in the end. Cook the meat until brown, about 4 to 5 minutes. While the sausage is browning, prepare the broccoli. Cut the broccoli tops into small florets. Remove the fibrous outer layer of the stem (just square it off using your knife), then thinly slice the tender center portion of the stem.

Once the sausage is brown, remove it to a paper-towel-lined plate. Return the skillet to the heat and add all of the broccoli and the chopped onion. Spread the veggies out in an even layer in the pan, season with some salt and pepper, and let the broccoli brown up a bit before stirring, about 2 minutes. Add the garlic and red pepper flakes and continue to cook 2 minutes more. Add the sausage back to the skillet along with the chicken stock. Ladle in some cooking water from the pasta and bring up to a simmer. Cook until the broccoli is tender and the liquids have reduced slightly, about 2 minutes. Add the lemon juice, parsley, and cooked, well-drained pasta. Toss to combine and simmer 1 last minute to allow the pasta to soak in the sauce and flavors. Turn the heat off, add the grated cheese, and toss to combine.

To serve, place a large dollop of the pepper-lemon-ricotta mixture into each of 4 shallow bowls and bury it with hot pasta. Once you are at the table, mix it up with a fork to distribute the ricotta cheese. Serve with extra grated cheese.

And make sure you have the following On Hand:

Salt • Short-cut pasta • Lemon • Black pepper • EVOO • Onion • Garlic • Red pepper flakes • Chicken stock • Flat-leaf parsley • Parmigiano-Reggiano or Pecorino Romano cheese

Chicken Sausage and Egg Sammies

Here's an easy B,L, or D (breakfast, lunch, or dinner) that you won't find on any take-out or diner menu!

MAKES 4 SAMMIES

  3 tablespoons **EVOO** (extra-virgin olive oil)
½ small **onion**, finely chopped
  2 large **jarred roasted red peppers**, well drained
  1 package **ground chicken**, about 1 pound
  1 tablespoon **grill seasoning**, such as McCormick's Montreal Steak Seasoning
¼ teaspoon ground **allspice**, eyeball it
  1 teaspoon **fennel seeds**
  4 large **eggs**
      Salt and **black pepper**
  4 slices **provolone cheese**
  4 crusty **Kaiser rolls**, sesame or plain, split

Place a medium nonstick skillet over medium heat and add 1 table-spoon EVOO, once around the pan. Add the onions to the hot pan and cook 2 to 3 minutes. While they cook, cut off one quarter of a roasted pepper and chop it finely. Add the chopped pepper to the onions and combine, then transfer to a medium bowl to cool.

EXPRESS LANE
SHOPPING LIST

❑ 1 pound ground chicken

❑ 4 slices Provolone cheese

❑ 4 sesame or plain Kaiser
   rolls

When the onions and pepper are cool, add the ground chicken, grill seasoning, allspice, and fennel seeds. Combine thoroughly then form the mixture into 4 large, thin patties. Return the skillet to the stove over medium-high heat and add another tablespoon of EVOO. Cook the patties until golden on both sides, 8 minutes total. Transfer the patties to a plate and tent with foil to keep them warm. Return the skillet to the heat. Add the remaining tablespoon of EVOO, reduce the heat to medium low, then add the eggs. Season the eggs with salt and pepper and fry for 2 to 3 minutes on the first side, then flip and cook to desired doneness, over easy to over hard. Top the eggs with a slice of provolone cheese just after you turn them and tent the pan with foil to melt the cheese.

Chop the remaining peppers in the food processor until smooth, then season with salt and pepper to taste.

Place a chicken sausage patty on each roll and top with a fried egg and cheese plus a rounded spoonful of roasted pepper puree. Set the roll tops in place and serve hot.

And make sure you have the following On Hand:

EVOO • Onion • Jarred roasted red peppers • Grill seasoning • Ground allspice • Fennel seeds • Eggs • Salt and black pepper

Mushroom Lovers' French Bread Pizzas

Mushrooms are beefy and delicious. This is a great quick supper for meat-free-ers and meat eaters alike because it is so hearty. To round out the meal, serve a simple green salad dressed with Dijon dressing or sliced apples or pears.

MAKES 4 12-INCH FRENCH BREAD PIZZAS

- 8 large **Portobello mushroom caps**
- 1 pound **button mushrooms**, stems trimmed
- 1/2 pound fresh **shiitake mushrooms**, stems discarded
- 3 tablespoons **EVOO** (extra-virgin olive oil), 3 times around the pan
- 2 tablespoons **butter**, cut into pieces
- 1 **bay leaf**
- 4 large **garlic cloves**, finely chopped
- **Salt** and **black pepper**
- 1/2 cup **dry white wine**, eyeball it
- 2 teaspoons **Worcestershire sauce**, eyeball it
- 1 tablespoon chopped fresh **thyme leaves**, 4 sprigs stripped and chopped
- 1 24-inch loaf of **crusty French bread**
- 3 cups shredded **Gruyère** or **Swiss cheese**

Preheat the broiler.

Wipe the mushrooms clean with a damp towel and slice them. Heat the EVOO and butter in a deep skillet over medium heat. When the butter melts into the oil, add the bay leaf, garlic, and sliced mushrooms. Cook until the mushrooms are dark and tender, 12 to 15 minutes. Season the mushrooms with salt and pepper and add the wine, stirring the skillet with a wooden spoon to deglaze. Shake the pan and add the Worcestershire and thyme. Turn off the heat.

Split the loaf first lengthwise and then across. Pull out and discard a bit of the soft insides. Toast the bread lightly under the broiler then fill each section of bread evenly with mushrooms. Top liberally with the cheese. Return the bread sections to the broiler until the cheese browns and bubbles then remove the pizzas from the oven and serve.

EXPRESS LANE SHOPPING LIST

- ❑ 8 large Portobello mushrooms
- ❑ 1 pound button mushrooms
- ❑ ½ pound fresh shiitake mushrooms
- ❑ 1 bunch fresh thyme
- ❑ 1 24-inch loaf French bread
- ❑ 1 pound Gruyère or Swiss cheese or 2 10-ounce sacks shredded

And make sure you have the following On Hand:

EVOO • Butter • Bay leaf • Garlic • Salt and black pepper • Dry white wine • Worcestershire

Wafflewiches

The Monte Cristo, a ham, turkey, and cheese sammie on French toast, is a fave of mine. This is guilty pleasure fun-and-tasty twist on the traditional 'Cristo.

MAKES 4 SAMMIES

2	tablespoons softened **butter**
4	tablespoons **honey mustard**
8	**waffles,** such as Eggos, lightly toasted
½	pound deli-sliced **ham**
½	pound deli-sliced **smoked turkey** or honey roast turkey
½	pound deli-sliced **Swiss cheese**
¾	cup prepared **cranberry sauce**

Heat a large nonstick skillet over medium heat. Add the butter and melt it. Assemble the sandwiches by spreading honey mustard on 4 of the waffles, then topping with equal amounts of ham, turkey, and Swiss cheese. Spread cranberry sauce liberally on the remaining 4 waffles and place them atop the sandwiches. Fry the assembled sandwiches in the melted butter and cook for a few minutes on each side until they are deeply golden in color and the cheese melts.

Bacon Bit Burgers with Smoked Gouda and Steak House Smothered Onions and Baby Spinach Salad

Bacon—what's not to like? It's smoky flavored salt and fat! Yum-o! In fact, the only way to improve on bacon is to wrap it up with beef and top it with cheese, then open wide! You gotta be more hungry than tired for this one!

4 SERVINGS

- 6 **smoky bacon slices**, chopped into ½ inch pieces
- 6 tablespoons **EVOO** (extra-virgin olive oil) plus more for for drizzling
- 2 yellow **onions**, ¼ finely chopped, 1¾ thinly sliced
- 1½ pounds **ground sirloin**
- 2 teaspoons **Worcestershire sauce**, eyeball it
- 1 teaspoon **hot sauce**, eyeball it
- 1 heaping tablespoon **grill seasoning**, such as McCormick's Montreal Steak Seasoning (a rounded palmful)
- 4 crusty **Kaiser rolls**, poppy seed or plain, split
- 4 slices **smoked Gouda**
- ¼ cup plus 1 tablespoon **steak sauce**, such as A-1 or Lea and Perrins
- 1 tablespoon **balsamic vinegar**
- 1 sack washed **baby spinach leaves**
   Salt and **black pepper**

Preheat the broiler and place a medium nonstick skillet over medium high heat.

Add the bacon and a drizzle of EVOO to the hot skillet and cook until crisp, 4 to 5 minutes. Transfer the bacon to a paper towel–lined plate and drain off all but 1 tablespoon or so of the fat from the skillet. Return the pan to medium low heat and add the finely chopped onions to sweat out in the remaining fat, 2 to 3 minutes.

Preheat a second medium nonstick skillet with 2 tablespoons of the EVOO, 2 times around the pan, over medium heat. When the oil is hot, add all the thinly sliced onions and top them with a plate that can fit inside the skillet. Top the plate with a heavy can and smother the onions for 10 minutes, stirring occasionally. Lift the plate with tongs; it'll be hot!

Place the beef in a bowl and top with the Worcestershire, hot sauce, and grill seasoning.

Remove the chopped onions to the plate with the bacon to cool. Turn off the heat and reserve the pan. Once the onions are cool, add them and the bacon to the ground sirloin and combine well. Score the meat into 4 even sections and form 4 large patties. Add 1 tablespoon of EVOO to the skillet and reheat it over medium high heat. Add the burgers and cook for 4 minutes on each side for medium rare, 6 minutes on each side for medium well.

Toast the split rolls under the hot broiler until golden. Place the burgers on the bun bottoms and top with the smoked Gouda. Remove the bun tops from the broiler pan. Return the burgers to the broiler just to melt the cheese, about 30 seconds.

Stir ¼ cup of the steak sauce into the smothered onions. Top the burgers with the onions and set the bun tops in place.

Place the remaining tablespoon of steak sauce in a small salad bowl. Add about 1 tablespoon of balsamic vinegar and whisk in about 3 tablespoons of EVOO. Toss with the spinach, season with salt and pepper, and serve alongside the burgers.

Provençal Vegetable Stew

I loved and still miss Julia Child. She consumed life as robustly as she did a good, crispy skinned chicken. If I had ever had her over for lunch, I would have made her this simple stew.

4 SERVINGS

¼ cup **EVOO** (extra-virgin olive oil), 3 to 4 times around the pan

4 **garlic cloves**, chopped

1 **bay leaf**

½ pound **button mushrooms**, trimmed and halved

1 yellow **onion**, chopped

2 **celery ribs**, chopped

1 **green** or **red bell pepper**, stemmed, seeded, and chopped

1 medium to large **eggplant**, cut in 1-inch cubes

Salt and **black pepper**

1 tablespoon fresh **thyme leaves**, chopped (a few sprigs)

1 tablespoon fresh **rosemary**, chopped (a couple of sprigs)

½ cup **dry white wine** (eyeball it)

1 14-ounce can **petite-diced tomatoes** or tomato sauce

Crusty bread, such as baguette

Heat the EVOO in a deep skillet over medium to medium high heat. Add the garlic, bay leaf, mushrooms, onions, celery, and peppers. Sauté for a couple of minutes, then add the eggplant and season everything with salt and pepper and the fresh herbs. Cook for 15 minutes or until the eggplant is tender. Deglaze with the wine and scrape up the vegetable bits from the bottom of the pan, then stir in the tomatoes or tomato sauce and heat through. Turn off the heat and discard the bay leaf. Let the vegetables stand a few minutes, then stir and serve with the warm crusty bread and butter.

BLT Soup

Bacon, Leek, and Tomato Soup is a soup for all seasons! So easy and too delicious; you'll make this one January or August, year after year. It is especially welcome on rainy nights.

4 SERVINGS

EVOO (extra-virgin olive oil) for drizzling

6 slices lean, smoky good quality **bacon**, chopped into ½-inch pieces

3 small **celery ribs** from the heart of the stalk, finely chopped

2 small to medium **carrots**

3 **leeks**, rough tops and roots trimmed

1 **bay leaf**

Salt and **black pepper**

3 medium starchy **potatoes**, such as Idaho, peeled

2 quarts **chicken stock**

1 14-ounce can **petite-diced tomatoes**, drained

A handful of **flat-leaf parsley**, finely chopped

Crusty bread, for dunking and mopping

Heat a medium soup pot or deep-sided skillet over medium-high heat. To the hot pan add a drizzle of EVOO and the bacon. Cook the bacon until brown and crisp. Remove the bacon to a paper towel–lined plate and reserve. Drain off all but 2 tablespoons of the remaining fat and add the chopped celery. While the celery cooks over medium heat, peel the carrots, then lay them flat on a cutting board. Hold each carrot at the root end and use the vegetable peeler to make long, thin strips. Chop the thin slices into small carrot bits or chips $\frac{1}{2}$-inch wide. Add the chips to the celery and stir. Cut the leeks lengthwise and then into $\frac{1}{2}$-inch half moons. Place the sliced leeks in a colander and run them under cold water, separating the layers to wash away all the trapped grit. When the leeks are clean, shake off the water and add to the celery and carrots. Stir the veggies together, add the bay leaf, and season with salt and pepper. While the leeks cook until wilted, 3 to 4 minutes, slice the potatoes.

Cut each potato into thirds crosswise. Stand each potato third upright and slice it thinly. The pieces will look like raw potato chips.

Add the stock to the vegetables and bring to a boil. Reduce the heat and add the potatoes and tomatoes. Cook for 8 to 10 minutes or until the potatoes are tender and starting to break up a bit. Add the reserved bacon and parsley and stir. Adjust the seasonings. Serve immediately with the crusty bread.

And make sure you have the following On Hand:

EVOO • Bacon • Celery • Carrots • Bay leaf • Salt and black pepper • Potatoes • Chicken stock • Canned diced tomatoes • Flat-leaf parsley

CHIVES 4888

CM PECORINO

5 @ 0.69

SCALLION4068

BOUNTY

B&G RSTD PPR

CENTO PEPPRS

MORTON SALT

BATAMPTE PCK

GROUND CHICK

AUST ALPS

PANCETTA

MEALS FOR THE NOT *TOO* TIRED

These are menus that involve some chopping, but not a lot of attention. They are low-stress and, like a food version of low-impact aerobics, these meals will help you keep your kitchen skills honed without breaking a sweat. Some of my favorites in this section include the Veal Sausage and Broccoli Rabe with Pasta and Sicilian Spaghetti with Fennel and Onion. (See a pattern here?) On the lighter side, check out the Teriyaki Chicken with Warm Ginger-Carrot Slaw or the Fabulous Baked Fish and Asparagus Spears.

Super Herbed Sautéed Salmon with Creamy Leeks and Bacon

Try halibut, mahi-mahi, or tilapia in this recipe, too. Leeks and bacon are so delish . . . add some fish and they become good for you, too.

4 SERVINGS

- 3 tablespoons **EVOO** (extra-virgin olive oil)
- 6 **bacon slices**, coarsely chopped
- 3 large **leeks**, superdark green parts and roots discarded
- 2 large **garlic cloves**, finely chopped
- ½ teaspoon **dried thyme** (eyeball it)
- 1 large pinch of **red pepper flakes**
  Salt and **black pepper**
- ¾ cup **white wine**, a few good glugs (eyeball it)
- 1½ cups **chicken stock**
- ¼ cup **half-and-half** or heavy cream (eyeball it)
- 4 6-ounce portions **salmon fillet**, skin removed
- ½ cup fresh **flat-leaf parsley**, chopped, a couple of handfuls
- 3 sprigs fresh **dill**, chopped
  Zest of 1 lemon
  Crusty bread to pass at the table

Preheat a large skillet over medium heat with 1 tablespoon of the EVOO, once around the pan. Add the chopped bacon and cook, stirring every now and then, until crisp, about 2 to 3 minutes. While the bacon is getting crisp, get the leeks ready.

To clean the leeks, cut each in half lengthwise, then thinly slice each half into half moons. Fill a large bowl with cold water, transfer the sliced leeks to the water, swish and swoosh the leeks around in the water, and then let them sit without messing with them for a minute. Using your hands, skim the leeks from the water without disturbing the grunge that has settled to the bottom. Drain the leeks thoroughly, feeling them for grit. If you feel some, repeat the cleaning process with a clean bowl of water. Don't forget to thoroughly wipe off your cutting board after chopping the leeks, otherwise the next thing you chop on the board will have sand and grit in it.

Once the bacon is crisp, remove it from the skillet to a paper-towel-lined plate and reserve. Don't wipe the skillet out; there is lots of bacon flavor in there. Return the skillet to the stovetop over medium heat and add the leeks, half the garlic, the thyme, red pepper flakes, salt, and pepper and cook, stirring occasionally, for 3 minutes. Add the white wine and cook for 1 minute, then add the chicken stock and half-and-half or heavy cream. Bring the mixture up to a simmer, then turn down the heat to medium low. Simmer the mixture for about 10 to 12 minutes, until tender and creamy.

While the leeks are cooking, start the salmon. Season the salmon on all sides with some salt and pepper. On a plate, combine the parsley, dill, the remaining garlic, and the lemon zest. Gently press one side of each salmon fillet into the herb mixture. Preheat a medium or large nonstick skillet over medium heat with the remaining 2 tablespoons of EVOO. Once the oil is hot, add the salmon fillets herb side down. Cook the salmon about 2 to 3 minutes on the herb side, then turn the heat up to medium high, flip the salmon, and continue to cook for 4 to 5 minutes, or until cooked through.

Add the reserved crispy bacon to the leeks and stir to combine. Divide the leeks among 4 serving plates. Top each pile of leeks with a portion of the salmon. Cut the lemon into wedges and squeeze the juice over the fish. Serve with some crusty bread on the side.

EXPRESS LANE SHOPPING LIST

- ❑ **3 large** leeks
- ❑ **4 6-ounce portions** salmon fillet
- ❑ **1 bunch fresh** dill
- ❑ **1 loaf** crusty bread

And make sure you have the following On Hand:

EVOO • Bacon • Garlic • Dried thyme • Red pepper flakes • Salt and black pepper • White wine • Chicken stock • Half-and-half or heavy cream • Flat-leaf parsley • Lemon

Fillets of Sole Francese and Lemon-Basil Pasta

SO easy! TOO delish! I make Chicken Francese all the time, but this recipe for Sole Francese is actually based on a fish sandwich served at The Algonquin on Lake George, New York. I have been eating this fish there, dockside in the summer sun, for more decades than I care to acknowledge. (See you there next year!)

4 SERVINGS

Salt

1 pound **long-cut pasta**, such as vermicelli or spaghetti

4 **sole fillets**, 7 to 8 ounces each

Black pepper

2 large **eggs**, beaten

3 tablespoons **half-and-half** or whole milk

3 tablespoons **butter**, cut into pieces

Zest and juice of 2 lemons

¼ cup **EVOO** (extra-virgin olive oil), 4 times around the pan

4 to 5 **garlic cloves**, finely chopped

½ cup **dry white wine**

1 cup fresh **basil**, about 20 leaves, shredded or torn

1 **plum tomato**, seeded and diced small

EXPRESS LANE
SHOPPING LIST

❑ 4 sole fillets, 7 to 8 ounces
  each

❑ 1 bunch fresh basil

❑ 1 plum tomato

Place a large pot of water on to boil for the pasta. Salt the boiling water, add the pasta, and cook it to al dente; it should still have a bite to it. Heads up: you will need to use a ladleful of the starchy cooking liquid for the sauce before you drain the pasta.

While the pasta cooks, rinse and pat the fish dry, then season with salt and pepper. Beat the eggs with the half-and-half or milk. Heat a large nonstick skillet over medium heat. Add the butter. When the butter has melted and is hot, dip the fillets in the egg mixture, then transfer them to the skillet. Cook the fillets for 3 to 4 minutes on each side, or until deeply golden brown.

And make sure you have
the following On Hand:

Salt • Long-cut pasta • Black
pepper • Eggs • Half-and-
half or whole milk • Butter
• Lemons • EVOO • Garlic •
White wine

While the fish cooks, zest the lemons. Heat the EVOO in a deep skillet over medium-low heat. Add the lemon zest and garlic to the EVOO. Sweat the garlic for 2 minutes, then add the wine and reduce for 30 seconds. Add a ladle of the starchy pasta water and the juice of 1 of the lemons and reduce for 30 seconds more. Turn off the heat.

When the fish is done, transfer it to serving plates and add the juice of the remaining lemon to the pan. Turn the heat off. Let the lemon juice combine with the pan juices, then spoon the juices over the fish.

Drain the pasta well and add to the garlic-lemon-wine sauce. Add the basil and toss the pasta for 1 minute to absorb the flavors. Season the pasta with salt and pepper. Serve the pasta alongside the fish garnished with cubes of plum tomato.

Salmon Burgers with Caesar Slaw

Wild Alaskan canned salmon is a great staple to keep on hand—it's packed with good nutrition and calcium. This is my favorite way to use it, but also try it scrambled up with eggs and sweet peas, or tossed with some cream, pasta, and fresh dill or tarragon. It's so versatile!

4 SERVINGS

1   14-ounce can Alaskan salmon, drained and flaked

2   egg whites, lightly beaten

    A handful of fresh flat-leaf parsley, finely chopped

    Zest and juice of 1 lemon

3   garlic cloves, finely chopped

¾   cup Italian bread crumbs, 3 generous handfuls

    Black pepper and salt

4   anchovies, finely chopped (optional)

2   teaspoons Dijon mustard

1   tablespoon Worcestershire sauce (eyeball it)

¼   cup EVOO (extra-virgin olive oil), plus 2 tablespoons

    A couple of handfuls of grated Parmigiano-Reggiano or
        Pecorino Romano cheese

2   romaine lettuce hearts, shredded

1   head radicchio, shredded

In a bowl, combine the flaked salmon, egg whites, parsley, the lemon zest, two thirds of the chopped garlic, the bread crumbs, and lots of black pepper and a little salt. Form 4 large patties or 8 mini patties.

Juice the lemon into a salad bowl—get it all! Add the remaining garlic, the chopped anchovies, Dijon mustard, and Worcestershire. Whisk in about ¼ cup EVOO and the cheese. Add lots of black pepper, no salt. Add the shredded lettuces to the bowl and toss to coat evenly. Now, season the slaw with salt to taste, if necessary.

Preheat the 2 tablespoons of EVOO, twice around the pan, in a nonstick skillet over medium to medium-high heat. Cook the salmon patties for 2 to 3 minutes on each side for mini patties, 4 minutes on each side for large patties.

Serve the salmon burgers atop a mound of the Caesar slaw.

And make sure you have the following On Hand:

Canned Alaskan salmon • Eggs • Flat-leaf parsley • Lemon • Garlic • Italian bread crumbs • Black pepper and salt • Anchovies (optional) • Dijon mustard • Worcestershire • EVOO • Parmigiano-Reggiano or Pecorino Romano cheese

Veal Sausage and Broccoli Rabe with Pasta

My "favorite" pasta changes each time I whip up a new one. Here I go again.

4 SERVINGS

Salt

1 pound **short-cut pasta**, such as penne

1 pound **ground veal**

2 tablespoons thinly sliced **sage leaves**, a couple of sprigs

1 teaspoon **fennel seeds**

3 **garlic cloves**, minced

1 small **onion**, finely chopped

½ teaspoon **red pepper flakes**

Black pepper

1½ pounds **broccoli rabe**, 1 large or 2 small bunches, trimmed and cut into bite-size pieces

2 tablespoons **EVOO** (extra-virgin olive oil)

A couple of handfuls of grated **Parmigiano-Reggiano** cheese, plus some to pass at the table

EXPRESS LANE
SHOPPING LIST

❏ **1 pound** ground veal

❏ **Fresh** sage leaves, **a couple
of sprigs**

❏ **1½ pounds** broccoli rabe,
**1 large or 2 small
bunches**

Bring a large pot of water to a boil for the pasta. Salt the water and cook the pasta to al dente. Heads up: you will need a ladle of the cooking water for the pasta sauce.

In a medium bowl, combine the veal, sage, fennel seed, garlic, onions, red pepper flakes, salt, and black pepper.

Bring an inch of salted water to a boil in a deep skillet. Add the broccoli rabe and boil for 7 to 8 minutes. Drain well.

Return the skillet to the stovetop and heat to medium-high heat. Add the EVOO and the veal sausage mixture and break it up. Cook the veal crumbles for 5 to 6 minutes, until lightly browned all over. Add the broccoli rabe and combine. Adjust the salt and pepper to taste.

Add a ladle of starchy pasta cooking water to the sausage and rabe, then drain the pasta and add to the skillet. Combine the pasta with the sausage and broccoli rabe. Add a couple of handfuls of grated cheese to the pan and adjust the salt and pepper one final time, then serve.

And make sure you have
the following On Hand:

Salt • Short-cut pasta •
Fennel seeds • Garlic • Onion
• Red pepper flakes • Black
pepper • EVOO •
Parmigiano-Reggiano cheese

Chicken Sausage, Pepper, and Onion Subs

I'm famous for my sausage sandwiches . . . my homemade relish is the secret that makes them great. Double the relish recipe and use it on any Italian cold cut sandwich. Either traditional Italian sweet or hot pork sausage will work fine in this.

MAKES 4 SUBS

- 4 **fresh chicken sausages**, available at the meat counter
- 3 tablespoons **EVOO** (extra-virgin olive oil)
- 1/3 cup **chicken stock** or dry white wine, a generous douse
- 1 **cubanelle pepper**, seeded and sliced
- 1 red **bell pepper**, seeded and sliced
- 1 large **onion**, thinly sliced
- 3 **garlic cloves**, chopped

    Salt and **black pepper**

- 1 cup **giardiniera** (Italian pickled vegetable salad; see Note)

    A handful of fresh **flat-leaf parsley**

- 1/2 cup fresh **basil**, 10 leaves

    Zest of 1/2 lemon

- 4 crusty **sub rolls**, split

> NOTE: Giardiniera is a mixture of pickled hot peppers, cauliflower, carrots, and celery. It's available in jars on the Italian foods aisle or in bulk bins near the olives.

Place the chicken sausages in a large skillet and add 1 inch of water. Prick the sausages. Add 1 tablespoon of the EVOO to the skillet, once around the pan. Bring the water to a boil, then reduce the heat a little. Allow all the liquid to cook away, then brown and crisp the casings, 10 to 12 minutes total. Deglaze the pan with the stock or wine and cook it off, 1 minute. Remove the sausages to a platter.

Add the remaining 2 tablespoons of EVOO to the skillet. Add the peppers, onions, and garlic, season with salt and pepper, and cook for 10 minutes, or until tender.

Place the giardiniera, parsley, basil, and lemon zest in a food processor and grind them into a relish.

Slice the sausages on an angle. Fill each roll with a little relish, then peppers and onions, then the sliced sausages.

EXPRESS LANE SHOPPING LIST

- ☐ 4 fresh chicken sausages, available at the meat counter
- ☐ 1 cubanelle pepper
- ☐ 1 red bell pepper
- ☐ 1 cup giardiniera (Italian pickled vegetable salad; see Note)
- ☐ 1 bunch fresh basil
- ☐ 4 crusty sub rolls

And make sure you have the following On Hand:

EVOO • Chicken stock or dry white wine • Onion • Garlic • Salt and black pepper • Flat-leaf parsley • Lemon

Red Snapper with Sweet Anchovy–Pine Nut Sauce and Caramelized Zucchini

This is my favorite fish dish in the book. Try it and you'll taste why.

4 SERVINGS

  6 tablespoons **EVOO** (extra-virgin olive oil)

  4 8-ounce portions **red snapper fillet**

    Salt and **black pepper**

  ¼ cup **pine nuts**, a generous handful

  2 medium **zucchini**, sliced in thin half moons

  ½ cup fresh **flat-leaf parsley**, a couple of handfuls, chopped

  2 large **garlic cloves**, chopped

  ½ tin **flat anchovy fillets**, drained

  1 large pinch **red pepper flakes**

  ½ cup **white wine**, a few good-size glugs

  1 cup **chicken stock**

  ½ cup **dried black currants**, a couple of handfuls

  2 tablespoons **heavy cream** or half-and-half, a good-size splash

Heat a large nonstick skillet over medium-high heat and coat with a tablespoon of EVOO, once around the pan.

With a sharp knife, score the skin side of each snapper fillet in a 1-inch crosshatch. Season both sides of the snapper with salt and pepper. Cook the fillets skin side down for 4 or 5 minutes, until the skin is crisp. Turn

EXPRESS LANE
SHOPPING LIST

❑ **4 8-ounce portions** red
    snapper fillet

❑ **¼ cup** pine nuts

❑ **2 medium** zucchini

❑ **Small box** dried black
    currants

the fillets and cook them on the reverse side for about 3 minutes, or until the fillets are firm and the flesh is opaque.

Preheat another skillet over medium-high heat (you will use this for both toasting the pine nuts and cooking the zucchini). Add the pine nuts and cook them until lightly toasted, about 2 to 3 minutes, stirring frequently. Remove the nuts from the skillet and reserve. Return the skillet to the stove over medium-high heat with 2 tablespoons of EVOO. Add the zucchini and season liberally with freshly ground black pepper and a little salt. Cook until the zucchini is lightly brown and tender, about 5 minutes. Once cooked, add half of the parsley and toss to distribute. If the zucchini is done before you are finished with the sauce for the snapper, simply cover the pan with a piece of foil to keep it warm.

**And make sure you have
the following On Hand:**

EVOO • Salt and black
pepper • Flat-leaf parsley •
Garlic • Anchovy fillets •
Red pepper flakes •
White wine • Chicken stock •
Heavy cream or half-and-half

Once the snapper is cooked, transfer the fish to a warm, shallow serving dish. Return the pan to the stovetop and reduce the heat to medium. Add the remaining 3 tablespoons of EVOO, then add the garlic, anchovies, and red pepper flakes. Sauté the mixture until the anchovies melt into the EVOO and dissolve completely and the garlic is tender, about 3 minutes. Add the wine and cook for 1 minute, then add the chicken stock, currants, and cream and continue to cook until the liquid is reduced by half, 2 minutes. Add the remaining parsley and the toasted pine nuts to the sauce. Give the sauce a taste for seasoning and adjust with salt and pepper. Arrange the zucchini on serving plates and top with the snapper fillets. Pour the sauce over the fish and serve.

Smoked Paprika Chicken with Egg Noodles and Buttered Warm Radishes

Just like Grandma might have made for you, if she were Hungarian.

4 SERVINGS

Salt

8 ounces **extra-wide egg noodles**

2 tablespoons **EVOO** (extra-virgin olive oil), twice around the pan

1½ pounds **chicken breast tenders**, cut into bite-size pieces

1 medium **onion**, thinly sliced

2 **garlic cloves**, chopped

1½ teaspoons **smoked sweet paprika**, ½ palmful

Black pepper

½ cup **chicken stock** (eyeball it)

2 tablespoons **butter**, cut into small pieces

1 pound large **radishes**, trimmed and halved

½ cup **sour cream** or reduced-fat sour cream

2 tablespoons chopped or snipped **chives** (eyeball it)

¼ cup fresh **flat-leaf parsley**, a generous handful, chopped

Bring a pot of water to a boil for the egg noodles. Salt the water and cook the noodles for 6 minutes, or until tender but with a little bite left to them.

Heat a large skillet over medium-high heat. Add the EVOO and then the chicken. Lightly brown the meat on all sides for 3 to 4 minutes. Add the onions and garlic and cook it for a few minutes more. Season the chicken mixture with the smoked paprika, salt, and pepper, then stir in the chicken stock and reduce the heat to low.

Heat a small skillet over medium to medium-high heat. Add a tablespoon of the butter and melt it. Add the radishes and cook for 3 to 4 minutes to warm through.

Stir the sour cream into the chicken and turn the heat off. Add the chives to the radishes and turn the heat off under this pan as well. Drain the noodles and return them to the warm pot. Add the remaining tablespoon of butter and toss to coat the noodles. Add half the parsley to the noodles. Divide them among 4 dinner plates. Top with the chicken and sauce and garnish with the remaining parsley. Serve the radishes alongside the chicken and noodles.

EXPRESS LANE SHOPPING LIST

- ❑ Extra-wide egg noodles (you need 8 ounces, or half a 1-pound sack)
- ❑ 1½ pounds chicken breast tenders
- ❑ 1 pound large radishes, any variety
- ❑ 8-ounce container sour cream or reduced-fat sour cream
- ❑ 1 bunch fresh chives

And make sure you have the following On Hand:

Salt • EVOO • Onion • Garlic • Smoked sweet paprika • Black pepper • Chicken stock • Butter • Flat-leaf parsley

Italian Tuna Casserole

Tuna casserole was a classic back in the day when I was a kid. I'm bringing it back—Mediterranean style!

4 SERVINGS

1 10-ounce box **frozen chopped spinach**

Salt

1 pound medium or large **shell pasta** or other short-cut pasta with ridges

1 tablespoon **EVOO** (extra-virgin olive oil), once around the pan

2 tablespoons **butter**, cut into pieces

1 medium **onion**, finely chopped

5 **garlic cloves**, finely chopped

3 tablespoons **all-purpose flour**

½ cup **dry white wine**, a couple of glugs

1 cup **chicken stock** (eyeball about ¼ of a quart-size box—the rest can go right in the fridge)

2 cups **milk**

¼ teaspoon freshly **grated nutmeg**, or to taste

1 teaspoon **hot sauce** (eyeball it)

1 teaspoon **Dijon mustard**

Black pepper

2 6-ounce cans **white tuna in water**, drained, or 3 4-ounce cans Italian tuna in oil, drained

1 cup grated **Parmigiano-Reggiano** or Pecorino Romano cheese, 3 very generous handfuls

A handful of chopped fresh **flat-leaf parsley**

EXPRESS LANE
SHOPPING LIST

❑ Go home! You have
everything you need.

Place the spinach on a plate and microwave it for 6 minutes on high to defrost it. Place it in a clean kitchen towel and wring it dry, then reserve.

While the spinach is defrosting, get a large pot of water on the stove for the pasta. Bring to a boil, then salt the water liberally and cook the shells to al dente.

While the pasta works, heat a deep, large skillet over medium heat. Add the EVOO, then melt the butter into the oil. When the butter melts, add the onions and garlic and cook until tender, 4 to 5 minutes. Sprinkle the flour around the pan and cook for a minute, then whisk in the wine—it will cook off and the mixture will thicken almost immediately. Whisk in the stock, then whisk in the milk and bring it to a bubble. Reduce the heat a bit. Season the sauce with the nutmeg, hot sauce, and mustard, then season with salt and pepper to taste. Simmer for 2 to 3 minutes to thicken, then add the spinach, separating it as you add it to the sauce.

Preheat the broiler.

Back to the sauce: add the tuna, flaking it as you go, then stir to combine. Heat the spinach and tuna through for a minute or so. Drain the pasta and toss with the sauce. Transfer the tuna to a casserole dish and cover it with the Parm or Romano. Place the casserole under the broiler for 2 minutes to brown the edges and the cheese. Top with the parsley and serve.

And make sure you have the following On Hand:

Frozen chopped spinach • Salt • Short-cut pasta with ridges, such as shells • EVOO • Butter • Onion • Garlic • Flour • White wine • Chicken stock • Milk • Nutmeg • Hot sauce • Dijon mustard • Black pepper • Canned white tuna or Italian tuna • Parmigiano-Reggiano or Pecrino Romano cheese • Flat-leaf parsley

Chicken Caesar Burgers
For Wade

Wade, my good friend and coworker for many years, joined me at a fancy restaurant in Las Vegas in honor of our friend Lucky's birthday. He saw me cringe as he politely asked our server to request that the chef prepare a "Chicken Caesar" for him. The broad menu of culinary creations just struck him as too complicated for a late-night-following-a-long-workday meal. I rolled my eyes and the server gave a bit of a twitch.

In hindsight, I have rarely been so ashamed of my own behavior: me, an Upstate New York blue-collar girl, suddenly acting too haughty to even sit with someone who would request a Chicken Caesar outside of a highway pit stop.

Chef Eric Klein at SW at the Wynn Las Vegas Hotel made Wade a fabulous free-range roast chicken Caesar salad. Eric was neither shocked nor insulted by the simple request. Instead, he made a humble visit to the table to remind us all of the Golden Rule of food: the customer is always right.

Wade, this burger is for you. Viva Chicken Caesar!

4 SERVINGS

1   package **ground chicken breast**

3   **garlic cloves**, 2 finely chopped, 1 cracked from the skin

4   **anchovies**, finely chopped (yes, Wade, they're optional—but recommended)

A couple of handfuls of grated **Parmigiano-Reggiano** or Pecorino Romano cheese

Salt and **coarse black pepper**

1   tablespoon **Worcestershire sauce**

A handful of fresh **flat-leaf parsley**, chopped

Zest of 1 lemon plus juice of ½ lemon

4   tablespoons **EVOO** (extra-virgin olive oil), plus some for drizzling

4 crusty rolls, split

1 teaspoon **Dijon mustard**

1 **romaine lettuce** heart, chopped

2 **plum tomatoes**, thinly sliced

Gourmet potato chips

EXPRESS LANE
SHOPPING LIST

❑ **1 package** ground chicken
breast **(1⅓ pounds is
the average weight)**

❑ **4** crusty rolls

❑ **1** romaine lettuce **heart**

❑ **2** plum tomatoes

❑ **1 sack** gourmet potato
chips, **any brand/flavor**

In a bowl, combine the ground chicken, finely chopped garlic, anchovies, a handful of the cheese, a pinch of salt, a generous amount of pepper, the Worcestershire, parsley, and lemon zest. Score the mixture and form 4 oval, rather than round, patties.

Heat a large nonstick skillet with 1 tablespoon of the EVOO, once around the pan, over medium-high heat. When hot, add the chicken patties and cook for 3 to 4 minutes on each side.

Preheat the broiler and toast the rolls on a cookie sheet or broiler pan. When they are lightly golden in color, remove the sheet from the oven and rub the breads with the cracked garlic clove. Drizzle the bread with EVOO and sprinkle with the remaining handful of cheese. Return the sheet to the broiler for another 30 seconds, then remove it and let it stand.

In a large bowl, combine the Dijon, lemon juice, and the remaining 3 tablespoons of EVOO with salt and pepper. Toss the romaine in the dressing.

Place the patties on the roll bottoms and top them with a pile of dressed romaine, sliced tomatoes, and the roll tops. Serve the burgers with chips alongside.

And make sure you have the following On Hand:

Garlic • Anchovies (optional) • Parmigiano-Reggiano or Pecorino Romano cheese • Salt and black pepper • Worcestershire • Flat-leaf parsley • Lemon • EVOO • Dijon mustard

Everything Lo Mein (MYOTO)

Make your own take-out. When you MYOTO, you control the salt, fat, and quality of ingredients. This dish is not only healthful, but you also don't have to make any decisions like whether you want chicken or pork. This recipe has got everything in it but the kitchen sink.

4 SERVINGS

3 rounded tablespoons hoisin sauce

3 tablespoons tamari (eyeball it)

2 teaspoons hot sauce (eyeball it)

Salt

1 pound spaghetti

4 tablespoons vegetable oil

2 large eggs, beaten

3 chicken breast cutlets, sliced into thin strips

3 thin-cut pork chops, sliced into thin strips

Black pepper

2 teaspoons ground coriander

4 garlic cloves, finely chopped

2-inch piece fresh ginger, peeled and finely chopped or grated

6 scallions, cut into 3-inch lengths, then sliced lengthwise

½ pound fresh shiitake mushrooms, stemmed and chopped

1 red bell pepper, cut into quarters, seeded, then sliced

1 small can sliced water chestnuts, chopped

2 cups fresh bean sprouts, 4 generous handfuls, or ½ pound packaged shredded cabbage

Mix together the hoisin, tamari, hot sauce, and about 3 tablespoons of water in a small bowl and reserve.

Bring a big pot of water to a boil for the pasta. Salt the water, add the pasta, and cook to al dente.

While the pasta cooks, heat 1 tablespoon of the vegetable oil, once around the pan, in a large, nonstick skillet over high heat. When the oil ripples, add the beaten eggs and scramble them to light golden brown. Remove to a plate and reserve.

Season the meat strips with salt, pepper, and the coriander. Heat the remaining 3 tablespoons of vegetable oil to a ripple over high heat, then add the meat and stir-fry for 4 minutes. Push the meat to the sides of the skillet and add the garlic, ginger, scallions, shiitakes, bell peppers, water chestnuts, and bean sprouts or cabbage. Stir-fry the veggies for 2 minutes, then add the drained pasta and the eggs to the skillet. Pour the reserved sauce over the lo mein and toss it to combine. Turn off the heat. Toss for 30 seconds and let the pasta absorb all of the liquids. Taste it to adjust the seasonings. Yum-o! You're not getting this off of any take-out menu!

EXPRESS LANE SHOPPING LIST

- ☐ **Small jar** hoisin sauce
- ☐ **3** chicken breast cutlets
- ☐ **3 thin-cut** pork chops
- ☐ **2-inch piece** fresh ginger
- ☐ **1 bunch** scallions
- ☐ **½ pound fresh** shiitake mushrooms
- ☐ **1 red** bell pepper
- ☐ **1 small can sliced** water chestnuts
- ☐ **4 generous handfuls fresh** bean sprouts, **or ½ pound packaged** shredded cabbage

And make sure you have the following On Hand:

Tamari • Hot sauce • Salt • Spaghetti • Vegetable oil • Eggs • Black pepper • Ground coriander • Garlic

Turkey Cutlets with Pumpkin-Pistachio Muffin Stuffin' and Chipotle Gravy

Make a Thanksgiving dinner, Southwestern style, any night of the year with this stuffing shortcut.

4 SERVINGS

- 3 tablespoons EVOO (extra-virgin olive oil)
- 4 tablespoons (1/2 stick) butter
- 1 medium onion, chopped
- 2 celery ribs, chopped
- 1 Golden Delicious apple, unpeeled, finely chopped
- 1 small yellow squash or 6 pattypan squash, chopped
  Salt and black pepper
- 1 teaspoon poultry seasoning
- 1 cup shelled natural pistachios, chopped
- 4 purchased pumpkin muffins
- 2 cups chicken stock
- 1 package turkey breast cutlets
- 2 tablespoons all-purpose flour
- 1/2 cup dry white wine or beer, whichever you have on hand
- 1 or 2 chipotle chilies in adobo, finely chopped
- 2 scallions, finely chopped

EXPRESS LANE
SHOPPING LIST

❑ **1** Golden Delicious apple

❑ **1 small** yellow squash **or 6 pattypan squash**

❑ **1 cup shelled natural** pistachios **(available in bulk foods section)**

❑ **4** pumpkin muffins

❑ **1 package** turkey breast cutlets **(1⅓ pounds is the average weight)**

❑ **1 bunch** scallions

Heat a large skillet over medium-high heat. Add 1 tablespoon of the EVOO, once around the pan, and 2 tablespoons of the butter. When the butter melts into the oil, add the onions, celery, apples, and squash. Season with salt, pepper, and poultry seasoning. Sauté the vegetables and fruit for 5 minutes. Add the chopped nuts and then crumble in all of the muffins. Moisten the stuffing with 1 cup of the chicken stock. Adjust the seasoning, turn off the heat, and reserve the stuffing, tented loosely with foil.

Heat a second large skillet over medium-high heat. Season the cutlets with salt and pepper. Add the remaining 2 tablespoons of EVOO to the skillet and cook the cutlets for 6 minutes on each side, or until golden and cooked through. Transfer the meat to a platter and cover it with foil. Add the remaining 2 tablespoons of butter to the skillet and reduce the heat to medium low. Add the flour to the butter and whisk together for 2 minutes, or until the flour smells nutty and the color is medium brown. Whisk in the wine or beer and cook it for 30 seconds. Whisk in the remaining cup of chicken stock and bring it to a bubble. Stir the chipotle and scallions into the gravy and season with salt.

To serve, top a mound of the muffin stuffin' with the turkey cutlets and a ladle or two of the gravy.

And make sure you have the following On Hand:

EVOO • Butter • Onion • Celery • Salt and black pepper • Poultry seasoning • Chicken stock • Flour • Dry white wine or beer • Canned chipotle chilies in adobo

Tuscan Calzones with "The Works"

Get in "The Zone." These calzones are meat-free, super hearty, and super healthy.
Eat up, chow down, and enjoy.

4 SERVINGS

1 sack (1 pound) pizza dough

   A little flour to dust your hands with

4 tablespoons EVOO (extra-virgin olive oil), plus some
   for drizzling

4 portobello mushroom caps, thinly sliced

3 garlic cloves, chopped

2 tablespoons chopped fresh rosemary

   Salt and black pepper

1 10-ounce box frozen chopped spinach

1 15-ounce can cannellini beans, drained

2 cups shredded provolone or mozzarella cheese

1 15-ounce can pizza sauce

¼ cup kalamata or oil-cured olives, pitted and finely chopped

Preheat a medium nonstick skillet.

Preheat the oven to 400°F. Cut the dough into 4 equal portions. Dust your hands with flour and spread the dough into 4 rounds, 8 to 10 inches in diameter.

To the hot skillet, add 2 tablespoons of the EVOO, twice around the pan, then add the sliced mushrooms and two thirds of the chopped garlic. Cook the mushrooms until they are dark and tender, 10 minutes, then season with rosemary, salt, and pepper.

While the mushrooms cook, microwave the frozen spinach on high for 6 minutes. Place the defrosted spinach in a clean kitchen towel and wring dry. Separate the spinach as you transfer it to a bowl with the drained beans. Mash the beans with the spinach and remaining chopped garlic, a drizzle of EVOO, and salt and pepper to taste.

Spread half of each dough round with one fourth of the bean mixture. Top with one fourth of the mushrooms and then about 1/2 cup of cheese. Fold the dough over and seal the calzones. Brush a cookie sheet with EVOO, arrange the calzones on the sheet, and brush the remaining EVOO lightly over each calzone. Bake the calzones until golden all over, 15 minutes.

Heat the pizza sauce over low heat in a small pot. Stir in the chopped olives and remove it from the heat.

Serve the calzones with small ramekins of black-olive pizza sauce for dipping.

EXPRESS LANE SHOPPING LIST

- ❑ **1 sack (1 pound)** pizza dough, **any brand**
- ❑ **4** portobello mushroom caps
- ❑ **Fresh** rosemary, **a couple of sprigs**
- ❑ **1 10-ounce sack** shredded provolone **or mozzarella cheese**
- ❑ **1 15-ounce can** pizza sauce, **any brand**
- ❑ **¼ cup** kalamata or oil-cured olives, **a large spoonful from the bulk bin**

And make sure you have the following On Hand:

Flour • EVOO • Garlic • Salt and black pepper • Frozen chopped spinach • Canned cannellini beans

Mikey from Philly Cheese Steaks

This is my make-at-home version of one of my favorite brunch items at Union Square Cafe in New York City. Chef Michael Romano makes a mean Italian-style hoagie with sliced steak, tomato sauce, and capers—yum-o! When I'm up at my cabin, out in the sticks, I gotta make a knockoff for myself. (Michael, aka Mikey here, isn't really from Philly. Rather I am referring to his riff on Philly's famous cheese-steak sammies.)

4 SERVINGS

1½ pounds **thick-cut sirloin**

4 tablespoons **EVOO** (extra-virgin olive oil), plus some for drizzling

Coarse salt and **coarse black pepper**

1 **red bell pepper**, seeded and sliced

1 large **onion**, quartered and sliced

5 **garlic cloves**, 3 chopped, 2 cracked from the skin

1 large loaf **ciabatta bread** or other chewy Italian loaf, split

½ cup grated **Pecorino Romano** cheese, a couple of generous handfuls

½ cup **dry red wine**

½ cup **beef stock**

1 cup **tomato sauce** or crushed tomatoes

3 tablespoons **capers**, drained and coarsely chopped

A fistful of fresh **flat-leaf parsley**, coarsely chopped

8-ounce chunk **sharp provolone cheese**

Slice the meat very thin with a sharp knife, working against the grain.

Heat 2 tablespoons of the EVOO, twice around the pan, in a large non-stick pan over high heat. When the oil ripples, add the meat slices and sear them for just a minute or two to caramelize evenly all over—keep the meat moving with tongs. Season the meat slices with salt and pepper, remove to a platter, and tent loosely with foil. Go 2 more times around the pan with the EVOO and reduce the heat a bit, to medium high. Add the peppers, onions, and chopped garlic, season with salt and pepper, and cook, stirring frequently, for 5 minutes.

Preheat the broiler to high and place the rack on the second highest position. Arrange the split loaf of bread on a broiler pan and toast until evenly golden. Once toasted, rub the bread with the cracked garlic cloves, drizzle with EVOO, and top with grated Pecorino Romano and a few grinds of black pepper. Slide the bread back under the broiler to melt the cheese, 45 seconds. Remove the bread and reserve, keeping the broiler on.

Add the wine to the softened vegetables and cook down for 1 minute. Add the stock, then the tomatoes, capers, and parsley and bring to a bubble. Slide the meat and any juices back into the pan to heat through for 2 to 3 minutes.

Shred the cheese with a box grater or slice thin. Pile the meat and vegetables evenly over the entire loaf of bread and cover with the provolone. Place the gi-gundo-size sandwiches under the broiler to melt the cheese until bubbly. Cut each open-faced sammy into 4 sections, transfer 2 to each plate with a large spatula, and serve.

EXPRESS LANE SHOPPING LIST

- ❑ **1½ pounds** thick-cut sirloin, **2½ inches thick**
- ❑ **1 red** bell pepper
- ❑ **1 large loaf** ciabatta bread **or other chewy Italian loaf**
- ❑ **8-ounce chunk** sharp provolone **cheese**

And make sure you have the following On Hand:

EVOO • Coarse salt and coarse black pepper • Onion • Garlic • Pecorino Romano cheese • Dry red wine • Beef stock • Canned tomato sauce or crushed tomatoes • Capers • Flat-leaf parsley

Sicilian Spaghetti with Fennel and Onion

This quick pasta has big flavors and lots of texture. Salty, sweet, crunchy—Delish!

4 SERVINGS

Salt
1 pound **spaghetti**
¼ cup **pine nuts**, a generous handful
6 tablespoons **EVOO** (extra-virgin olive oil)
1 cup **bread crumbs**
1 rounded teaspoon **coarse black pepper**, ⅓ palmful
¼ cup chopped fresh **flat-leaf parsley**, a generous handful
5 **garlic cloves**, finely chopped
1 2-ounce tin **flat anchovy fillets**, drained (about 8 fillets)
½ teaspoon **red pepper flakes** (eyeball it)
1 large **fennel bulb**, tops trimmed, a handful of fronds reserved
1 large **onion**, very thinly sliced
¼ cup **golden raisins**, a generous handful, chopped
½ cup **dry white wine**, a couple of good glugs

Bring a large pot of water to a boil over high heat. When the water boils, salt it and add the pasta. Cook the spaghetti to al dente. Heads up: you will need to reserve a ladle of the pasta cooking liquid before you drain the pasta.

EXPRESS LANE
SHOPPING LIST

❑ ¼ cup pine nuts, a
   generous handful

❑ 1 large fennel bulb

❑ ¼ cup golden raisins, a
   generous handful

Heat a small skillet over medium heat. Add the pine nuts and toast them until golden. Remove the nuts and add 3 tablespoons of the EVOO to the same skillet, 3 times around the pan. Heat the oil, then add the bread crumbs and toast them. When they are deeply golden all over, remove them from the heat and season them with a little salt and lots of coarse black pepper, about a teaspoon. Add the parsley and nuts to the bread crumbs and toss to combine.

Heat the remaining 3 tablespoons of EVOO in a large nonstick skillet over medium heat. Add the garlic, anchovies, and red pepper flakes. As they heat, the anchovies will melt into the EVOO. Stir them in with the back of a wooden spoon.

Trim the fennel bulb of its tough outer skin. Quarter the fennel bulb lengthwise and cut out the core with an angled slice. Thinly slice the trimmed, quartered bulb lengthwise.

Add the fennel and sliced onions to the skillet and sauté in the garlic-anchovy oil until they are tender but not caramelized, 5 minutes. Add the chopped golden raisins and the wine to the skillet and reduce for a minute or so. Add a ladle of the cooking liquid from the pasta water to the skillet, then drain the pasta and add it to the sauce. Toss the spaghetti with half the bread crumbs and add salt to taste. Serve the pasta immediately and pass the remaining bread crumbs at the table to sprinkle over the pasta as you would grated cheese.

And make sure you have the following On Hand:

Salt • Spaghetti • EVOO • Bread crumbs • Coarse black pepper • Flat-leaf parsley • Garlic • Anchovy fillets • Red pepper flakes • Onion • Dry white wine

Bread Pizza Stuffed with Meat and Mushrooms

French bread pizza from Stouffer's was my favorite frozen food as a kid. Now that I'm all grown up I make my own, because I can overstuff them. (My appetite grew, too.)

4 SERVINGS

1   18- to 24-inch loaf **Italian semolina bread** (day-old is fine)

3   tablespoons **EVOO** (extra-virgin olive oil)

4   medium **portobello mushroom caps**, thinly sliced

2   slices **pancetta** or bacon, chopped

2   pounds **ground beef**

2   medium **yellow onions**, finely chopped

1   **carrot**, grated or finely chopped

    Coarse black pepper and **coarse salt**

1   tablespoon **Worcestershire sauce**

1   teaspoon **ground allspice**, 1/3 palmful

1/2   cup **red wine**, a couple of glugs

1/2   cup **beef stock**

1   14-ounce can **crushed tomatoes**

    A handful of fresh **flat-leaf parsley**, finely chopped

1   pound **fresh mozzarella**, thinly sliced

1   handful grated **Parmigiano-Reggiano** or Pecorino Romano cheese

1   cup fresh **basil**, 20 leaves, shredded or torn

Heat the oven to 350°F. Split the bread lengthwise, then cut it in half again and hollow out some of the soft insides of the bread. Lightly crisp the bread in the oven, 10 minutes. Remove the bread and switch the broiler on.

Heat a medium nonstick skillet over medium-high heat. Add 2 tablespoons of the EVOO, twice around the pan, and the mushrooms. Cook the mushrooms until dark and tender, 7 to 8 minutes, stirring frequently.

Heat a second medium nonstick skillet over medium-high heat with the remaining tablespoon of EVOO. When the EVOO smokes, add the pancetta or bacon and render the fat for a minute or so, then add the ground beef and break it up into an even layer. Deeply brown and caramelize the meat, 5 minutes. Add the onions and carrots and season with lots of coarse pepper, some salt, the Worcestershire, and the ground allspice, then cook for 10 minutes more, stirring frequently. Add the wine and scrape up all the brown bits. Add the stock to loosen up the mixture a little, then add the tomatoes and parsley and heat through, 1 to 2 minutes. Remove from the heat.

Season the cooked mushrooms with salt and pepper. Fill the toasted breads with equal amounts of mushrooms, then top them with equal amounts of the meat sauce. Cover the meat sauce with a layer of mozzarella and a sprinkle of Parmigiano or Romano cheese. Broil the pizzas to melt the cheese. Shred or tear the basil and top each pizza liberally with it, then serve (with a fork and knife).

EXPRESS LANE SHOPPING LIST

- ❑ **1 18- to 24-inch loaf** Italian semolina bread **(day-old is fine)**

- ❑ **4 medium** portobello mushroom caps

- ❑ **2 slices** pancetta **(or use bacon that you have on hand)**

- ❑ **2 pounds** ground beef

- ❑ **1 pound** fresh mozzarella, **smoked, regular mozzarella, or scamorza (firmer, aged mozzarella balls)**

- ❑ **1 bunch fresh** basil

And make sure you have the following On Hand:

EVOO • Onions • Carrot • Coarse black pepper and coarse salt • Worcestershire • Ground allspice • Red wine • Beef stock • Canned crushed tomatoes • Flat-leaf parsley • Parmigiano-Reggiano or Pecorino Romano cheese

Turkey Sausage Burgers with Peppers and Onions

When they're made with 99 percent lean ground turkey breast, these burgers are a figure-friendly way to enjoy a sausage sandwich.

4 SERVINGS

- 1 package ground turkey breast
- 1 teaspoon fennel seeds, 1/3 palmful
- 3 garlic cloves, 2 finely chopped, 1 cracked from the skin

  Salt and black pepper

  A couple of handfuls grated Parmigiano-Reggiano or Pecorino Romano cheese

  A handful of fresh flat-leaf parsley, finely chopped
- 1 teaspoon red pepper flakes, 1/3 palmful
- 2 tablespoons EVOO (extra-virgin olive oil)
- 1 red bell pepper, seeded and sliced
- 2 cubanelle peppers, seeded and sliced
- 1 large onion, sliced
- 4 crusty rolls, split
- 1/4 pound deli-sliced provolone cheese

  Gourmet potato chips

In a medium bowl, combine the turkey, fennel, chopped garlic, salt and pepper, grated cheese, parsley, and red pepper flakes. Mix well and form 4 patties.

Heat 2 nonstick skillets over medium-high heat, add a tablespoon of EVOO, once around the pan, to each pan, and preheat the broiler.

Add the patties to one skillet and the peppers and onions to the other. Cook the patties for 3 to 4 minutes on each side. Cook the peppers and onions until tender, 6 to 7 minutes. Season the peppers and onions with salt and pepper.

Place the split rolls on a cookie sheet or broiler pan and toast the cut sides under the broiler. Rub the toasted surfaces with the cracked garlic.

Arrange the provolone slices evenly over the patties in the skillet, then loosely tent the skillet with foil to melt the cheese in the last minute or so. Place the cheesy sausage burgers on the roll bottoms. Top them with mounds of peppers and onions and the roll tops. Serve with a few chips.

Monday Night Football Food
Taco Bowls

When you're watching the big game it's important to have some smashmouth, tough-guy food like this.

4 SERVINGS

- 1 sack **tortilla chips**
- 3 tablespoons **EVOO** (extra-virgin olive oil)
- 2 pounds **ground beef**
- 2 **jalapeño peppers**, seeded and finely chopped
- 2 medium **onions**, chopped
- 3 to 4 **garlic cloves**, chopped
- 1½ tablespoons **ground cumin**, a rounded palmful
- 1½ tablespoons **chili powder**, a rounded palmful
- **Coarse salt** and **black pepper**
- 2 firm **Hass avocados**
- 4 **plum tomatoes**, seeded and chopped
- A handful of fresh **cilantro leaves**, chopped
- **Juice of 1 lemon**
- 4 cups shredded **Monterey Jack** or sharp Cheddar cheese

Lightly crush the chips by popping open the bag and giving the chips a few light whacks with a frying pan. Careful that they don't fly out of the sack—hold the bag loosely at the top with one hand while you crush the chips with the other.

Heat a large nonstick skillet over medium-high heat. Add 2 tablespoons of the EVOO, twice around the pan. Add the beef to the skillet and brown and crumble it for 5 minutes. To the browned meat add half the chopped jalapeño, three fourths of the chopped onions, and all of the garlic. Season the meat with the cumin, chili powder, and salt and pepper. Cook them together for 5 minutes more, then add about a cup of water and reduce the heat to low. Add salt to taste.

Halve and separate the avocados. Remove the pit with a spoon. Use a small knife to dice the avocado while still in the skin. Scoop out the diced flesh and place it in a bowl. Combine the tomatoes, remaining onions, remaining jalapeño, and the cilantro gently with the avocado and dress the salad with the lemon juice, the remaining tablespoon of EVOO, and salt to taste.

Layer a handful or two of the chips into soup or chili bowls and top them with a handful of cheese. Fill the bowls with taco meat and top with more cheese, then mound some salad on top and serve.

EXPRESS LANE SHOPPING LIST

- [ ] **1 sack** tortilla chips, **any brand or color (yellow, blue, red, white)**
- [ ] **2 pounds** ground beef
- [ ] **2 jalapeño peppers**
- [ ] **2 firm Hass avocados**
- [ ] **4 plum tomatoes**
- [ ] **1 bunch fresh** cilantro
- [ ] **2 10-ounce sacks shredded Monterey Jack or sharp Cheddar cheese**

And make sure you have the following On Hand:

EVOO • Onions • Garlic • Ground cumin • Chili powder • Coarse salt and black pepper • Lemon

Crab and Corn Chowda-Mac

Though I haven't lived on Cape Code since I was eight, this dish proves I'm not just a Red Sox fan but a true New England Patriot. With Chowda *and* Mac 'n' Cheese in one dinner, you can get to Massachusetts in 30 minutes or less, even if you live in Michigan.

4 SERVINGS

Salt

1 box **large shell pasta**

1 tablespoon **EVOO** (extra-virgin olive oil), once around the pan

3 **bacon slices**, chopped

1 medium **onion**, chopped

2 **celery ribs** with greens, chopped

½ small red **bell pepper**, cored, seeded, and chopped

2 tablespoons **all-purpose flour**

1 cup **chicken stock**

1 cup **milk**

1 6-ounce tub **fresh lump crab meat**, flaked

1 cup **frozen corn kernels**

2 cups shredded sharp white **Cheddar cheese**

2 tablespoons fresh **thyme**, chopped

A couple of pinches **cayenne pepper**

3 tablespoons chopped or snipped fresh **chives**, for garnish

Bring a large pot of water to a boil for the pasta and salt it. Cook the pasta to al dente.

While the pasta cooks, heat a large, deep skillet over medium to medium-high heat. Add the EVOO and the bacon. Cook the bacon for 3 minutes. Add the onions and celery and cook for 3 minutes more. Add the bell peppers and cook for another minute or two. Add the flour and cook for 1 to 2 minutes. Whisk in the stock, then the milk. When the milk bubbles, add the crab and corn to heat through, another minute. Stir in the cheese, thyme, and cayenne pepper and heat until the cheese melts into the sauce. Drain the pasta and toss with the cheese, crab, and corn sauce. Adjust the seasonings. Ladle into bowls and garnish with the chives.

Fabulous Baked Fish and Asparagus Spears

This is one of my mom's recipes so it's better than good . . . it's the best.

4 SERVINGS

  2 tablespoons **EVOO** (extra-virgin olive oil)

  1 teaspoon **fennel seeds**, 1/3 palmful

  4 **garlic cloves**, chopped

  1 **shallot**, sliced

  2 pounds **haddock fillets**

    Salt and **black pepper**

  2 tablespoons **capers**, drained

  1 14-ounce can **diced tomatoes**

  2 tablespoons **balsamic vinegar** (eyeball it)

1/2 cup fresh **basil**, 10 leaves, torn or shredded

1/2 cup **clam juice**

    Crusty bread, for mopping

  1 pound thin **asparagus**, tough ends trimmed

    Juice of 1/2 lemon

EXPRESS LANE
SHOPPING LIST

❑ **2 pounds** haddock fillets
❑ **1 bunch** fresh basil
❑ **1 8-ounce** bottle clam juice
❑ **1 loaf** crusty bread
❑ **1 pound** thin asparagus

Preheat the oven to 400°F.

Heat a large ovenproof nonstick skillet on the stovetop over medium heat. Add 1 tablespoon of the EVOO to the pan, once around the pan. Add the fennel seeds, garlic, and shallots to the pan and cook for 2 minutes.

Rinse the fish fillets and pat them dry. Season the fish with salt and pepper, and set aside.

In a small bowl, combine the capers, tomatoes, the remaining tablespoon of EVOO, the balsamic vinegar, basil, and clam juice. Add the mixture to the skillet and cook for 2 to 3 minutes. Slide the fish fillets into the pan. Spoon the sauce over the fish and transfer the skillet to the oven. Bake the fish for 15 minutes, or until cooked through, adding the bread to the oven to warm through for the last minute or two.

While the fish cooks, boil the asparagus in an inch of water for 3 minutes, then drain and dress it with a little lemon juice and a pinch of salt.

Serve the fish with lots of juice for mopping up with crusty bread and the asparagus spears alongside.

And make sure you have the following On Hand:

EVOO • Fennel seeds • Garlic • Shallot • Salt and black pepper • Capers • Canned diced tomatoes • Balsamic vinegar • Lemon

Teriyaki Chicken with Warm Ginger-Carrot Slaw

This dinner is full of antioxidants, low in fat, high in fiber, and huge on flavor. Can you get anything better for you than that? Plus, you won't find this one on any take-out menu.

4 SERVINGS

1½   pounds **chicken breast cutlets**

⅓   cup **teriyaki sauce**

4   tablespoons **vegetable oil** (eyeball it)

1   rounded tablespoon **grill seasoning**, such as McCormick's Montreal Steak Seasoning (eyeball it in your palm)

1   small **Savoy cabbage**, about 1½ pounds

1   bunch **scallions**, trimmed

1   cup **snow peas**, a couple of handfuls

¼   cup **honey** (eyeball it)

3   tablespoons **cider vinegar** (eyeball it)

3   tablespoons **pickled ginger**, drained and thinly sliced (found on the Asian foods aisle)

2   cups shredded or julienned **carrots**

   Salt and **black pepper**

In a large plastic food storage bag, combine the chicken cutlets with the teriyaki sauce, 2 tablespoons of the oil, and the grill seasoning. Close the bag and press to coat the chicken evenly. Let the chicken stand for 15 minutes.

Preheat an outdoor grill or indoor grill pan or skillet to medium high.

Cut the cabbage into quarters and cut away the core. Shred the cabbage with a knife and set it aside. Cut the scallions into 3-inch lengths, then pile them lengthwise and julienne them into thin strips. Pull the threads from the ends of the snow peas and julienne them into thin strips, lengthwise, like the scallions.

Drizzle the honey into a small bowl. Add the vinegar and combine with a fork. Pat the chicken cutlets dry and place them on the grill or grill pan (or into a hot skillet) and cook for 3 minutes on each side.

Heat a nonstick skillet over high heat. Add the remaining 2 tablespoons of oil, twice around the pan. Add the pickled ginger and the carrots and stir-fry for 2 minutes. Add the cabbage and stir-fry for 2 minutes more. Fluff and toss the veggies with tongs so they stay dry and crisp while cooking. Add the scallions and snow peas and stir-fry for another minute. Add the honey and vinegar combination, pouring it all around the pan in a slow stream. Cook the liquids down for 30 seconds, then turn off the heat. Continue to toss the slaw and season it up with salt and pepper to taste.

Thinly slice the chicken on the diagonal. Mound up one fourth of the slaw on each plate and place the sliced chicken alongside, edging its way up the slaw salad. Serve immediately.

EXPRESS LANE SHOPPING LIST

- [ ] 1½ pounds chicken breast cutlets
- [ ] 1 small bottle teriyaki sauce
- [ ] 1 small Savoy cabbage, about 1½ pounds
- [ ] 1 bunch scallions
- [ ] 8 ounces snow peas, a couple of handfuls
- [ ] 1 small jar pickled ginger (found on the Asian foods aisle)
- [ ] 1 10-ounce sack shredded or julienned carrots or peel and shred 4 medium carrots from your On Hand supply

And make sure you have the following On Hand:

Vegetable oil • Grill seasoning • Honey • Cider vinegar • Salt and black pepper

Chicken with Leek and Lemon-Poppy Muffin Stuffin' with Pucker-Up Pan Gravy Broth

This is one of my fancy fake-out meals. It looks like it came out of an Asian-influenced bistro, but the difference between your Express Lane receipt and your dinner check, not to mention the prep time, is substantial.

4 SERVINGS

- 2 medium leeks
- 2 tablespoons EVOO (extra-virgin olive oil), twice around the pan
- 4 tablespoons (½ stick) butter
- 2 celery ribs with leafy tops, chopped
- 4 lemon–poppy seed muffins
- 3 to 4 fresh thyme sprigs, leaves stripped and chopped

  Zest and juice of 1 lemon
- 1 teaspoon poultry seasoning, ⅓ palmful
- 2 cups chicken stock
- 8 chicken breast cutlets

  Salt and black pepper
- 2 tablespoons all-purpose flour

  A handful of fresh flat-leaf parsley, chopped, for garnish

Cut off the tough tops of the leeks, leaving 3 to 4 inches of greens. Trim the root ends and halve the leeks lengthwise. Thinly slice the leeks into half moons and transfer them to a colander. Run the leeks under cold water and separate all of the layers, freeing the sand and grit. Drain the clean sliced leeks well.

Heat a medium nonstick skillet over medium to medium-high heat with the EVOO, and 2 tablespoons of the butter. When the butter has melted, add the leeks and celery. Sauté the veggies for 5 minutes, then crumble the lemon–poppy seed muffins into the pan. Toast the muffin crumbles with the veggies for 3 to 4 minutes. Season the stuffing with the fresh thyme, lemon zest, and poultry seasoning. Moisten the stuffing with up to 1 cup of the chicken stock and reduce the heat to low.

While the stuffing works, heat a second skillet over medium-high heat. Season the chicken with salt and pepper and cook for 3 to 4 minutes on each side, then transfer it to a platter and cover it with foil to keep it warm. Add the remaining 2 tablespoons of butter to the pan and when it melts sprinkle the flour into the pan. Stir and cook for 1 minute, then whisk in the remaining cup of the chicken stock. Cook for 2 minutes, or until thickened. Whisk in the lemon juice and season with salt and pepper.

Pile up stuffing on 4 plates. Top with 2 pieces of chicken cutlets and ladle gravy over the top. Garnish with chopped parsley.

Road to Morocco Lamb with Pine Nut Couscous

You can make this dish again, subbing cubed white or dark meat chicken for the lamb if you have extra spice blend on hand.

4 SERVINGS

2½ pounds boneless **leg of lamb** cut in bite-size pieces

1 rounded tablespoon **grill seasoning**, such as McCormick's Montreal Steak Seasoning, a rounded palmful

2 teaspoons **ground cumin**, ⅔ palmful

1½ teaspoons **ground coriander**, ½ palmful

1½ teaspoons **paprika**, ½ palmful

1 teaspoon **turmeric**, ⅓ palmful

½ teaspoon **cinnamon** (eyeball it in your palm)

3 tablespoons **EVOO** (extra-virgin olive oil), 3 times around the pan

2 medium **onions**, thinly sliced

3 **garlic cloves**, chopped

20 to 24 **pitted dates**, halved, about 1 cup

1 quart **chicken stock**

2 tablespoons **butter**

3 tablespoons **pine nuts**, a generous palmful

2 cups plain **couscous**

4 **scallions**, chopped, for garnish

A handful of fresh **cilantro** leaves, finely chopped, for garnish

> ### TIDBIT
> Make a double or triple batch of this spice blend to use with ground chicken or turkey for an unexpected Moroccan burger. The spice blend will keep for 6 months in an airtight container.

Place the lamb in a resealable food storage bag. Combine the spices in a small bowl, then sprinkle them into the bag and seal the bag. Shake to coat the lamb pieces evenly in the spices.

Heat a large, deep skillet over medium-high to high heat. Add the EVOO, then the lamb. Sear and caramelize the lamb, turning to brown all sides, 5 to 7 minutes in all. Add the onions and garlic and cook for 5 minutes more. Add the dates and 2 cups of the chicken stock to the pan and cover. Cook for 7 to 8 minutes more to plump the dates and soften the onions. Remove the cover and adjust the seasonings.

During the last 5 minutes the lamb cooks, melt the butter in a saucepan. Add the pine nuts and stir until toasted, 1 or 2 minutes. Add the remaining 2 cups of stock and bring it to a boil. Remove the pan from the heat, add the couscous, and cover the pan. Let it stand for 5 minutes. Remove the lid and fluff the couscous with a fork.

Serve the lamb over the couscous in shallow dishes and garnish it with chopped scallions and cilantro.

EXPRESS LANE SHOPPING LIST

- ❑ 2¹/₂ pounds boneless leg of lamb
- ❑ 1 small jar turmeric
- ❑ 20 to 24 pitted dates, about 1 cup
- ❑ 1 small container pine nuts or 2 ounces from the bulk bin
- ❑ 1 bunch scallions
- ❑ 1 bunch fresh cilantro

And make sure you have the following On Hand:

Grill seasoning • Ground cumin • Ground coriander • Paprika • Cinnamon • EVOO • Onions • Garlic • Chicken stock • Butter • Plain couscous

Ginger Flank Steak with Wasabi Smashed Potatoes and Seared Savoy Cabbage

This is not your average steak and baked dinner; it's about meat and potatoes in a whole new way. Try the same recipe with beef cut for London Broil or skirt steaks. All of these cuts are affordable, but with this exotic recipe they become way above average.

4 SERVINGS

3-inch piece **fresh ginger**, peeled and grated

¼ cup **tamari**

Zest and juice of 2 limes

5 tablespoons **vegetable oil**

2 tablespoons **grill seasoning**, such as McCormick's Montreal Steak Seasoning

2 pounds **flank steak**

2½ to 3 pounds **Idaho potatoes** (4 large potatoes), peeled and cut into chunks

Salt

¼ to ⅓ cup **heavy cream**

1 to 2 tablespoons **wasabi paste**—how hot do ya like it?

4 **scallions**, root end trimmed

A handful of fresh **cilantro leaves**

1 small head **Savoy cabbage**, quartered, cored, and shredded with a knife

Black pepper

❑ 3-inch piece fresh ginger

❑ 2 pounds flank steak

❑ 1 tube prepared wasabi
   paste

❑ 1 bunch scallions

❑ 1 bunch fresh cilantro

❑ 1 small head Savoy
   cabbage (about
   1½ pounds)

Preheat a grill pan or outdoor grill to high.

Combine the ginger, tamari, lime juice, 3 tablespoons of the oil, and the grill seasoning in a large shallow dish. Add the meat to the marinade and turn to coat it. Let it stand for 10 minutes, then grill the meat for 6 to 7 minutes on each side.

Place the potatoes in a pot and cover them with water. Bring them to a boil, salt the potatoes, and cook them until tender, 10 to 12 minutes. Drain the potatoes and return them to the hot pot. Mash the potatoes, adding the cream and wasabi to achieve the desired consistency and heat level. Adjust the salt to taste.

While the potatoes and meat cook, finely chop the scallions together with the cilantro and lime zest. Set aside.

Heat a large skillet over high heat. Add the remaining 2 tablespoons of vegetable oil, twice around the pan. Stir-fry the cabbage until it's wilted and just tender but still has a bite, 4 to 5 minutes. Season the cabbage with salt and black pepper.

Let the meat rest for 5 minutes, then thinly slice it on an angle against the grain. Serve the meat on mounds of mashed potatoes and garnish with a generous sprinkling of the chopped scallion-cilantro-lime zest. Pile the seared cabbage alongside.

And make sure you have the following On Hand:

Tamari • Limes • Vegetable oil • Grill seasoning • Idaho potatoes • Salt • Heavy cream • Black pepper

Thai Chicken Pizza

Do you have trouble making up your mind? How does this sound: grilled meat, salad, take-out Thai food, and pizza, all in one meal? There are no special ingredients required; you can get them all in the regular market and have this pizza on the table in less time than it would take the delivery man to get to your door.

2 TO 4 SERVINGS

- 1 **pizza dough**
- ½ cup **duck sauce** or plum sauce
- ½ teaspoon **red pepper flakes**
- 1 10-ounce sack (2 cups) shredded **provolone** or Monterey Jack cheese
- ½ red **bell pepper**, cored, seeded, and thinly sliced
- 1 tablespoon **vegetable oil**
- 2 tablespoons **tamari**
- 1 rounded tablespoon smooth **peanut butter**
- 2 teaspoons **hot sauce**
- 2 teaspoons **grill seasoning**, such as McCormick's Montreal Steak Seasoning (eyeball it)
- 4 **chicken breast cutlets**, ½ pound total
- 2 tablespoons **honey**
- 2 tablespoons **cider vinegar** or any white vinegar on hand
- ¼ seedless **cucumber**, peeled and cut into matchsticks
- 4 **scallions**, white and green parts, chopped
- 1 cup **bean sprouts**, a couple of handfuls
  A palmful of fresh **cilantro leaves**, chopped
- ¼ cup **chopped roasted peanuts**

> **TIDBIT**
> If you use a 13.7-ounce tube of refrigerator pizza dough you'll get one rectangular pizza; if you prefer to stretch your own into a circle, use up to a 1-pound ball of fresh dough.

Preheat the oven to 425°F. Form the pizza crust on a pizza pan or cookie sheet. Top it with duck or plum sauce, spreading it around like you would pizza sauce. Sprinkle the pizza with some red pepper flakes, then top it with the cheese and bell peppers. Bake until golden and bubbly, 15 to 17 minutes.

In a small bowl, combine the vegetable oil, tamari, and peanut butter with the hot sauce and grill seasoning. Use the microwave to loosen up the peanut butter if it is too cold to blend into sauce; 10 seconds ought to do it. Coat the chicken evenly with the mixture and let it stand for 10 minutes. Preheat a grill pan or nonstick skillet over medium-high heat. Cook the chicken cutlets for 2 to 3 minutes on each side, or until firm. Slice the chicken into very thin strips.

While the chicken cooks, mix the honey and vinegar in a medium bowl. Add the cucumber and turn to coat in the dressing.

When the pizza comes out of the oven, top it with the chicken, scallions, sprouts, and cilantro. Drain the cucumbers and scatter them over the pizza. Garnish the pizza with peanuts, cut it into 8 wedges, and serve.

EXPRESS LANE SHOPPING LIST

- ❑ 1 pizza dough, fresh or in a 13.7-ounce tube
- ❑ 1 small jar duck sauce or plum sauce
- ❑ 1 10-ounce sack shredded provolone or Monterey Jack cheese
- ❑ 1 red bell pepper
- ❑ 4 chicken breast cutlets, ½ pound total
- ❑ 1 seedless cucumber
- ❑ 1 bunch scallions
- ❑ A couple of handfuls fresh bean sprouts
- ❑ 1 bunch fresh cilantro
- ❑ 1 small jar roasted peanuts

And make sure you have the following On Hand:

Red pepper flakes • Vegetable oil • Tamari • Peanut butter • Hot sauce • Grill seasoning • Honey • Cider vinegar or any white vinegar

Roasted Portobello Burgers with Rosemary Garlic Oven Fries

This sammy is so hearty you won't think to ask "where's the beef?"

4 SERVINGS

- 2 to 2½ pounds red or white **boiling potatoes**, washed
- 3 tablespoons **EVOO** (extra-virgin olive oil), plus some for drizzling
- 2 fresh **rosemary** sprigs, leaves finely chopped

  Salt and **black pepper**
- 2 tablespoons finely **chopped garlic**
- 8 large **portobello mushrooms**, stems removed
- 2 tablespoons **balsamic vinegar** (eyeball it)
- 4 cups **arugula leaves**, washed
- 2 jarred **roasted red peppers**, seeded
- 4 slices **prosciutto di Parma**
- 4 slices fresh **mozzarella cheese**

Preheat the oven to 450°F.

Cut the potatoes into wedges and drop them onto a cookie sheet. Drizzle the potatoes with about 3 tablespoons of EVOO and toss to coat them thoroughly in the oil. Season the potatoes with the rosemary, salt, and pepper. Roast them for 25 minutes in all. Halfway through the roasting add the garlic, stir to distribute, and flip the potatoes, then continue to roast. The potatoes should be brown and tender.

While the potatoes roast, place the portobello mushroom caps on a cookie sheet. Season them with salt and pepper and arrange the mushrooms gill side up. Drizzle the gill side with a little EVOO and the balsamic vinegar. Transfer them to the oven and roast for 12 minutes, or until they are cooked through. Don't turn off the oven.

While the mushrooms are roasting, coarsely chop the arugula and roasted red peppers and combine them in a bowl. Season them with a little salt and pepper.

Top 4 of the cooked mushroom caps with a mound of the arugula and roasted pepper mixture, a slice of prosciutto, and a slice of mozzarella. Return the mushrooms to the oven to melt the cheese, about 2 to 3 minutes. Once the cheese has melted, remove the mushrooms from the oven and top each one with a second roasted mushroom cap to make a sandwich. Serve the roasted portobello burgers with the rosemary garlic oven fries. It's easiest to eat these burgers with a fork and knife.

EXPRESS LANE
SHOPPING LIST

☐ **Fresh** rosemary, **2 sprigs**

☐ **8 large** portobello mushrooms

☐ **2 bunches** arugula **or 4 big handfuls from a bulk bin**

☐ **4 slices** prosciutto di Parma

☐ **1 ball fresh** mozzarella

And make sure you have the following On Hand:

Red or white boiling potatoes • EVOO • Salt and black pepper • Garlic • Balsamic vinegar • Jarred roasted red peppers

Grilled Chicken Hoagies with Mango Chutney and Melted Brie Served with Tomato Cucumber Salad

I love sandwiches because they are one-stop shopping: meat, salad, and cheese, all stuffed into bread. Oooooh-la-la, this is one fancy French grinder. Vive la Hoagie.

4 SERVINGS

- 5 tablespoons EVOO (extra-virgin olive oil), plus some for drizzling
- 1 teaspoon dried thyme, 1/3 palmful
- 2 garlic cloves, finely chopped
- Salt and black pepper
- 8 chicken breast cutlets
- 1 tablespoon Dijon mustard (eyeball it)
- 2 tablespoons white wine vinegar (eyeball it)
- 1 shallot, finely chopped
- 1 pint grape tomatoes, halved
- 1 English or European seedless cucumber, cut in half lengthwise, then thinly sliced into half moons
- 4 hoagie rolls (sub rolls)
- ¾ cup store-bought mango chutney
- 8 ounces Brie cheese, cut into thin slices
- 1 bunch watercress, trimmed and coarsely chopped

Heat a grill pan or outdoor grill to high heat.

In a shallow dish, mix together 2 tablespoons of the EVOO, the thyme, garlic, salt, and pepper. Add the chicken cutlets and coat thoroughly. Let the chicken marinate while you get the salad together and grill up the bread.

In a mixing bowl, combine the mustard, white wine vinegar, shallots, and a little salt and pepper. In a slow, steady stream, whisk in the remaining 3 tablespoons of EVOO. Add the grape tomatoes; with a fork smash some of the tomatoes against the side of the bowl so that their juices become part of the dressing. Add the sliced cucumbers and toss them to combine.

Cut the hoagie rolls in half lengthwise like a book, without separating the two halves all the way. Drizzle the inside of the rolls with some EVOO, hinge the rolls open, and lay them down on the grill with the inside flat against the grill. Once they are well marked, 1 to 2 minutes, flip them over and grill the outside a little bit. Remove the rolls from the grill and reserve.

Grill the cutlets for 3 to 4 minutes on one side. Flip the cutlets and top each with some of the mango chutney, spreading it out a bit, and 2 slices of Brie. Tent the chicken with a piece of foil and continue to grill it for 3 to 4 minutes to melt the cheese. Remove the cutlets from the grill, cut each in half, and distribute the chicken among the grilled rolls, wedging it into the bread. Top the chicken with some of the chopped watercress and squeeze the hoagies shut. Serve the sandwiches alongside the tomato cucumber salad.

EXPRESS LANE
SHOPPING LIST

❑ 8 chicken breast cutlets, about 1½ pounds
❑ 1 pint grape tomatoes
❑ 1 English or European seedless cucumber
❑ 4 hoagie rolls (sub rolls)
❑ 1 small jar mango chutney
❑ 8 ounces Brie cheese
❑ 1 bunch watercress

And make sure you have the following On Hand:

EVOO • Dried thyme • Garlic • Salt and black pepper • Dijon mustard • White wine vinegar • Shallot

Ginger Chicken and Sweet-Salty Noodles with Veggies

Sweet *and* salty food . . . I can eat it at the same time? I'm there. How about you?

4 SERVINGS

Salt

1 pound thin **long-cut pasta**, such as capellini

5 tablespoons **vegetable oil**

½ cup fresh **flat-leaf parsley**, a couple of handfuls

½ cup fresh **cilantro leaves**, a couple of handfuls

1 large **garlic clove**, smashed

¼ large **onion**, cut into chunks

3-inch piece **fresh ginger**, peeled and grated

Black pepper

1⅓ to 1½ pounds **chicken breast cutlets**, 8 thin pieces

½ cup mild **vinegar**, such as rice or white wine vinegar (eyeball it)

1½ rounded tablespoons **sugar**, 1½ palmfuls

3 tablespoons **tamari** (eyeball it)

¼ teaspoon **red pepper flakes** (eyeball it)

1 seedless **cucumber**, cut in half lengthwise, then thinly sliced into half moons

1 red **bell pepper**, cored, seeded, and thinly sliced

1 yellow **bell pepper**, cored, seeded, and thinly sliced

3 **scallions**, thinly sliced

1 12-ounce sack triple-washed **baby spinach**

Preheat a grill pan or outdoor grill on high.

Bring a large pot of water to boil for the pasta, salt the water, and add the pasta. Cook according to package directions until it is al dente. Once cooked, drain it thoroughly—get all the liquid out.

In a blender or food processor, combine about 3 tablespoons of the vegetable oil, the parsley, cilantro, garlic, onion, ⅔ of the grated ginger, and salt and pepper. Blend until the mixture is somewhat smooth. Transfer the mixture to a shallow dish, add the chicken cutlets, and coat them thoroughly. Let the chicken sit for a few minutes.

While the pasta cooks and the chicken marinates, place a small saucepan over medium-high heat, add the rice wine vinegar, sugar, tamari, red pepper flakes, and the remaining grated ginger and bring them up to a bubble to dissolve the sugar. Once the sugar has dissolved, remove the sauce from the heat and stir in the remaining 2 tablespoons of vegetable oil. While it is still hot, transfer the sauce to a large salad bowl, add the cucumbers, red and yellow bell peppers, and scallions, and toss to combine.

Add the pasta to the dressed cucumbers and bell peppers, add the baby spinach, and toss to combine. Cover with foil and reserve covered to keep the noodles warm and wilt the spinach while you grill up the chicken.

Grill the ginger-and-herb-coated chicken for 3 minutes on each side, or until it is cooked through and the juices run clear. Transfer the hot grilled chicken to a cutting board and cut it into thin strips. Divide the noodles and veggies among 4 serving plates and top them with a pile of the grilled chicken strips.

EXPRESS LANE SHOPPING LIST

- ❑ **1 bunch fresh** cilantro
- ❑ **3-inch piece** fresh ginger
- ❑ **1⅓ to 1½ pounds** chicken breast cutlets, **8 thin pieces**
- ❑ **1 English or European seedless** cucumber
- ❑ **1 red** bell pepper
- ❑ **1 yellow** bell pepper
- ❑ **1 bunch** scallions
- ❑ **1 12-ounce sack triple-washed** baby spinach

And make sure you have the following On Hand:

Salt • Long-cut pasta, such as capellini • Vegetable oil • Flat-leaf parsley • Garlic • Onion • Black pepper • Vinegar • Sugar • Tamari • Red pepper flakes

Flank Steak Salad with Grilled Croutons and Horseradish Dressing

This meal is high protein and high fiber, so it gets high marks.

4 SERVINGS

- 4 garlic cloves, 1 smashed and 3 chopped
- 1/3 cup plus 2 tablespoons **EVOO** (extra-virgin olive oil), plus some for drizzling
- 3 tablespoons **Worcestershire sauce** (eyeball it)
- 1 to 2 teaspoons **hot sauce** to taste (eyeball it)
- 1 teaspoon **dried thyme**, 1/3 palmful
- 2 pounds **flank steak**
- 5 thick slices of crunchy **peasant-style bread** such as ciabatta
  Salt and black pepper
- 1 rounded tablespoon **prepared horseradish**
  Juice of 1 lemon
- 3 tablespoons **sour cream** (eyeball it)
- 1 tablespoon **Dijon mustard**
- 1 pint **grape** or **cherry tomatoes**, halved
- 1 12-ounce sack triple-washed **baby spinach**
- 1 bunch **arugula**, thoroughly washed and dried

EXPRESS LANE
SHOPPING LIST

❏ **2 pounds** flank steak

❏ **1 loaf crunchy** peasant-style bread **such as ciabatta**

❏ **1 small jar** prepared horseradish

❏ **1 small container** sour cream

❏ **1 pint** grape **or** cherry tomatoes

❏ **1 12-ounce sack triple-washed** baby spinach

❏ **1 bunch** arugula

Preheat an outdoor grill, grill pan, or a large skillet (if you are using a large skillet for the steak, you might have to cut the steak in half in order to make it fit in the pan).

In a large shallow dish, combine the chopped garlic, about 2 tablespoons of the EVOO, the Worcestershire sauce, hot sauce, and thyme. Add the flank steak and coat it completely in the mixture; marinate it for 5 to 10 minutes, depending on how much of a rush you are in.

Brush or drizzle the bread slices with a little EVOO and sprinkle them with a little salt and pepper. Place the seasoned bread on the grill and grill on both sides until well marked, 1 to 2 minutes on each side. Remove the bread from the grill and rub it with the smashed garlic clove while still hot. Chop the grilled bread into 1-inch pieces and reserve it. (If you are not grilling, then simply toast the bread until it is golden brown and follow the same procedure.)

Season the flank steak with salt and pepper, then cook it for 5 to 6 minutes per side. Remove it from the grill and let it rest for 5 minutes. Thinly slice the flank steak on an angle and against the grain.

While the steak is grilling, in a small bowl combine the horseradish, lemon juice, sour cream, mustard, salt, and pepper. In a slow, steady stream, whisk in about ⅓ cup of EVOO.

In a large shallow platter or bowl, arrange the tomatoes, spinach, and arugula and top with croutons. Dress with about two thirds of the dressing. Toss the salad, then adjust the salt and pepper. Top the salad with the sliced steak and drizzle the remaining dressing over the meat.

And make sure you have the following On Hand:

Garlic • EVOO •
Worcestershire • Hot sauce •
Dried thyme • Salt and black
pepper • Lemon • Dijon
mustard

Dinner, Wrapped Up
Black Bean, Chicken, and Chorizo Burritos

This one reminds me of the California surfer scene. It's a way-cool mega-rito, dude!

4 SERVINGS

- 2 tablespoons vegetable oil
- 1 large onion, chopped
  Salt and black pepper
- 1½ cups white rice
- 3½ cups chicken stock
- ⅓ pound chorizo, chopped (a package usually weighs ¾ pound—use half)
- 3 large garlic cloves, chopped
- 2 teaspoons ground cumin, ⅔ palmful
- 1 teaspoon ground coriander, ⅓ palmful
- 1¼ to 1½ pounds chicken tenders, chopped into small dice
- 1 ripe Hass avocado
- 1 pint grape tomatoes, halved
- 1 small jalapeño pepper, seeded and finely chopped
- ¼ cup fresh cilantro leaves, a generous handful, chopped
  Juice of 1 lime
- 1 14-ounce can black beans, drained and rinsed
- 8 10- to 12-inch flour tortillas
- 2 cups shredded sharp Cheddar cheese
- ¾ cup prepared salsa (optional)
- 1 cup sour cream (optional)

Heat a medium-size saucepan with a tight-fitting lid over medium heat with about 1 tablespoon of the oil, once around the pan. Add one fourth of the chopped onion and season with salt and pepper, then cook for 1 minute. Add the rice, stir to coat in the oil, then add 2½ cups of the chicken stock and bring up to a simmer. Cover the pot, reduce the heat to medium low, and cook the rice for 15 to 17 minutes, until tender.

While the rice is cooking, preheat a large skillet over medium-high heat with the remaining tablespoon of vegetable oil. Add the chorizo and cook for 2 minutes. Add the remaining chopped onion, the garlic, cumin, coriander, and a little salt and pepper, and cook for about 3 minutes, or until the onions start to get tender. Add the chicken and cook for 4 to 5 minutes, or until the chicken is cooked through.

Halve the avocado, remove the pit with a spoon, and then carefully scoop out the flesh. Cut the two halves into small bite-size pieces and transfer to a bowl. Add the halved tomatoes, jalapeño, cilantro, lime juice, salt, and pepper, and mix to combine.

Add the remaining cup of chicken stock to the skillet with the chorizo and chicken and bring it up to a bubble. Once it is simmering, add the black beans and continue to cook until the liquids are just barely visible and the beans are heated through, a couple of minutes.

Heat a large dry skillet over high heat to blister the tortillas. Have a clean kitchen towel nearby to wrap the tortillas and keep them warm. Once the skillet is hot, add a tortilla and heat for about 30 seconds on each side, remove from the skillet, and wrap it in the towel. Continue until all the tortillas have been heated. If you have a gas stove, you can blister them directly over the flame itself.

Once the rice is done, fluff it with a fork. To assemble a burrito, scatter a small handful of cheese, about ¼ cup, across the center of a tortilla. Top with a couple of generous kitchen spoonfuls, about ¾ cup, of cooked rice. The rice will catch the juices from the couple of kitchen spoonfuls of black beans, chicken, and chorizo that come next! Dot the mound of fillings with some salsa and sour cream, if you like. Tuck the sides in, then wrap and roll. Cut in half and serve. Repeat to form up to 8 wraps.

EXPRESS LANE
SHOPPING LIST

❑ ⅓ pound chorizo

❑ 1¼ to 1½ pounds chicken tenders

❑ 1 ripe Hass avocado

❑ 1 pint grape tomatoes

❑ 1 small jalapeño pepper

❑ 1 bunch fresh cilantro

❑ 1 package 10- to 12-inch flour tortillas (burrito size)

❑ 1 10-ounce sack shredded sharp Cheddar cheese

❑ ¾ cup prepared salsa (optional)

❑ 1 8-ounce container sour cream (optional)

And make sure you have the following On Hand:

Vegetable oil • Onion • Salt and black pepper • White rice • Chicken stock • Garlic • Ground cumin • Ground coriander • Lime • Canned black beans

Bacon-Wrapped Halibut with Seared Cherry Tomato Sauce and Smashed Peas

Fancy? Yup! Got people you need to impress? Invite them over . . . you'll get the raise. Then you won't be *so* tired.

4 SERVINGS

- 4 6-ounce halibut fillets
  Salt and black pepper
- 8 center-cut bacon slices
- 3 tablespoons EVOO (extra-virgin olive oil)
- 2 tablespoons butter
- 1 small onion, finely chopped
- 2 10-ounce boxes frozen peas
- ¼ cup fresh flat-leaf parsley, chopped, a generous handful
  Zest of 1 lemon
- 3 tablespoons half-and-half or heavy cream (eyeball it)
- 1 pint cherry tomatoes
- 1 large garlic clove, chopped
- ¼ cup white wine, a good-size glug
- ¼ cup chicken stock, plus another ¼ cup to reheat peas if necessary (eyeball it)
- ½ cup fresh basil, about 10 leaves, chopped or torn

Season the halibut fillets with salt and pepper, going easy on the salt. Arrange 2 bacon slices side by side, overlapping slightly. Place one end of a halibut fillet on the edge of the bacon slices. Working in a spiral fashion, wrap and roll the bacon around the fish, pulling gently on the bacon to make both ends end up on the same side of the fillet. (This will prevent the bacon from unraveling as it cooks.) Reserve the fish in the fridge while you get the smashed peas working.

To a medium saucepan over medium heat, add 1 tablespoon of the EVOO, once around the pan, then 1 tablespoon of the butter and the onions. Sauté the onions for 2 minutes, then add the frozen peas, and raise the heat a bit. Stir the peas to heat them through and allow the liquid to evaporate. When the peas are heated through, add half of the parsley, the lemon zest, half-and-half or cream, salt, and pepper to the pan and smash it all together using a potato masher or fork. Turn the heat off and cover the peas with a lid or some foil to keep them warm.

Preheat a large nonstick skillet over medium heat with 1 tablespoon of the EVOO. Add the bacon-wrapped halibut to the hot skillet, bacon-end side down first, and cook them for 2 or 3 minutes on each of the 4 sides. Don't turn the fillets until the bacon is crispy looking on each side.

While the halibut cooks, start the seared cherry tomato sauce. Preheat a small skillet over high heat with the remaining tablespoon of EVOO; once it is screaming hot add the cherry tomatoes, season them with salt and pepper, and sear them for 1 minute without moving them. Turn the heat down to medium and shake the pan, add the garlic, and continue to cook for 1 minute. Next, add the white wine and cook until it has almost completely evaporated, then add ¼ cup of chicken stock. Bring the sauce to a bubble and remove it from the heat. Add the basil and the remaining tablespoon of butter and stir them to combine and melt the butter.

If the smashed peas need to be reheated, put the pot over medium heat, add ¼ cup of chicken stock, and stir until the peas are steaming.

To serve, spoon a portion of the smashed peas in the center of a dinner plate, arrange a bacon-wrapped halibut fillet on top of the peas, and top it with some of the seared cherry tomato sauce and the remaining parsley.

EXPRESS LANE SHOPPING LIST

- ❏ **4 6-ounce** halibut fillets
- ❏ **1 pint** cherry tomatoes
- ❏ **1 bunch fresh** basil

And make sure you have the following On Hand:

Salt and black pepper • Bacon • EVOO • Butter • Onion • Frozen peas • Flat-leaf parsley • Lemon • Half-and-half or heavy cream • Garlic • White wine • Chicken stock

Chorizo Chicken Spinach Stoup with Roasted Red Pepper and Manchego Toasts

Here's a killer dinner that even a charging Pamplona bull would brake for. Olé!

4 SERVINGS

- 2 tablespoons EVOO (extra-virgin olive oil), twice around the pan
- ½ pound chorizo, cut in quarters lengthwise, then thinly sliced
- 1 large yellow onion, chopped
- 3 garlic cloves, chopped
- Salt and black pepper
- 2 10-ounce boxes frozen chopped spinach
- 1 quart chicken stock
- ½ cup heavy cream or half-and-half
- ¾ pound chicken tenders, cut into bite-size pieces
- 8 baguette slices, cut ½ inch thick on an angle
- ⅓ pound manchego cheese, rind removed, grated
- 1 jarred roasted red pepper, chopped
- ¼ cup fresh flat-leaf parsley, a generous handful, chopped

EXPRESS LANE
SHOPPING LIST

❑ ½ **pound** chorizo

❑ ¾ **pound** chicken tenders

❑ **1** baguette

❑ ⅓ **pound** manchego
cheese

Heat a medium soup pot over medium-high heat with the EVOO. Add the chorizo and cook for about 2 to 3 minutes, stirring it frequently. Remove it from the pot to drain on a paper towel. To the hot soup pot add the onions, garlic, salt, and pepper. Cook while stirring frequently for about 4 or 5 minutes, or until the onions are tender and have taken on a little color.

Defrost the spinach in the microwave on high for 6 minutes. Place the spinach in a kitchen towel and wring out the liquid. Add the spinach to the onions and continue to cook for about 2 minutes. Transfer the onions and spinach to a blender or food processor with ½ cup of the chicken stock. Puree it until somewhat smooth. (If the pureeing gives you any trouble, add some more stock to get it going.) Add the pureed spinach back to the soup pot and stir in the remaining 3½ cups of chicken stock and the cream. Bring it up to a simmer and add the reserved chorizo and bite-size chicken pieces. Simmer them gently for 8 to 10 minutes, or until the chicken is cooked through and the flavors have come together.

Preheat the broiler and place a rack on the second groove. While the soup is simmering, toast the baguette slices until they are golden brown under the broiler. Mix the grated manchego with the roasted red pepper and the parsley on your cutting board. Once the toast is nice and golden, top each with a little of the cheese mixture and return them to the broiler or toaster oven to melt and lightly brown the cheese.

Transfer the stoup to serving bowls and serve 2 roasted pepper and manchego toasts alongside.

> **And make sure you have the following On Hand:**
>
> EVOO • Onion • Garlic • Salt and black pepper • Frozen chopped spinach • Chicken stock • Heavy cream or half-and-half • Jarred roasted red pepper • Flat-leaf parsley

Chicken Dumpling and Noodle Stoup

If you have a mini meatball in your house (or you're just a kid at heart) this one will feed you well, stomach and soul!

4 SERVINGS

Salt

½ pound **short-cut pasta**, such as ditalini or penne

2 tablespoons **EVOO** (extra-virgin olive oil), twice around the pan

1 large yellow **onion**, ¾ of it thinly sliced, ¼ of it grated

¼ teaspoon **red pepper flakes**, a couple of pinches

3 **garlic cloves**, chopped

Black pepper

5 cups **chicken stock**

1 package **ground chicken breast meat**

1 cup fresh **basil**, 20 leaves, chopped

¼ cup fresh **flat-leaf parsley**, a generous handful, chopped

1 **egg white**

Zest of 1 lemon

½ cup grated **Parmigiano-Reggiano** or Pecorino Romano cheese, a couple of handfuls, plus some to pass at the table

1 pint **grape tomatoes**

1 12-ounce sack triple-washed **baby spinach**

¼ cup store-bought **pesto**

Bring a medium pot of water to a boil, salt it, and cook the pasta just shy of al dente—about 5 minutes. Drain and reserve.

While the pasta works, preheat a large soup pot with the oil over medium-high heat. Add the sliced onion, red pepper flakes, garlic, salt, and pepper and cook, stirring frequently, for 4 to 5 minutes, until the onions are tender and golden. Add the chicken stock and bring it up to a boil, then turn down the heat to medium low and simmer while you make the chicken dumplings.

In a mixing bowl, combine the ground chicken, basil, parsley, egg white, grated onion, lemon zest, grated cheese, and a little salt and pepper. Mix well. Using a serving spoon, scoop out a walnut-size spoonful of the chicken mixture, then use a second serving spoon to push the chicken mixture off the first spoon into the simmering stock. Repeat this with the rest of the chicken mixture, working as quickly as you can to get all the balls into the stock. Shake the pan in order to settle the chicken dumplings into the stock. Cover and cook the dumplings for 5 minutes. Add the tomatoes, pasta, and spinach to the soup and cook for 2 minutes more. Ladle the soup into serving bowls and top each bowl with a dollop of the pesto and more grated cheese.

EXPRESS LANE
SHOPPING LIST

❑ 1 package ground chicken breast meat (1⅓ pounds is the average weight)

❑ 1 bunch fresh basil

❑ 1 pint grape tomatoes

❑ 1 12-ounce sack triple-washed baby spinach

❑ ¼ cup good-quality pesto, from the refrigerated section of the supermarket

And make sure you have the following On Hand:

Salt • Short-cut pasta • EVOO • Onion • Red pepper flakes • Garlic • Black pepper • Chicken stock • Flat-leaf parsley • Egg • Lemon • Parmigiano-Reggiano or Pecorino Romano cheese

Fish Tacos with Avocado Dressing

This dish is preventative medicine; it prevents one from ordering and pigging out on bad Mexican-style take-out food. If you make this instead you won't end up feeling too fat or too full.

4 SERVINGS

9	tablespoons **EVOO** (extra-virgin olive oil)
1	teaspoon **chili powder**, ⅓ palmful
	Zest and juice of 2 limes
	Salt
4	fresh **halibut steaks** or fillets, 6 to 8 ounces each
1	large yellow **onion**, chopped
3	large **garlic cloves**, chopped
1	**jalapeño pepper**, seeded and chopped
	Black pepper
1	10-ounce box **frozen corn kernels**
½	cup **chicken stock**
1	**romaine heart**, shredded
¼	cup fresh **cilantro leaves**, a generous handful, coarsely chopped
2	ripe **Hass avocados**
2	tablespoons **red wine vinegar** (2 splashes—eyeball it)
	A couple shakes of **hot sauce**, to taste (optional)
12	6-inch soft **flour tortillas**

In a shallow dish, combine 2 tablespoons of the EVOO, the chili powder, the juice of 1 lime, and a little salt. Add the halibut and coat with the mixture. Let the fish marinate while you start the corn.

Preheat a large skillet over medium-high heat with 2 tablespoons of the EVOO, twice around the pan. Add the onions, garlic, jalapeño, and a little salt and pepper. Cook for about 3 minutes, stirring frequently. Add the corn and chicken stock, bring it up to a bubble, then continue to cook for 2 minutes. Put the romaine and cilantro in a salad bowl, transfer the hot corn mixture to the bowl, and mix them together so the heat from the corn wilts the romaine. Wipe the skillet clean and return it to the stovetop over medium-high heat with 2 tablespoons of the EVOO. Once hot, add the halibut to the skillet and cook it on each side for 4 to 5 minutes, or until cooked through. Flake the fish into large chunks with a fork, then add it to the bowl with the corn and romaine.

While the fish is cooking, make the avocado dressing. Cut all around the ripe avocados down to the pit. Twist and separate the halved fruit. Remove the pit with a spoon, and then use a spoon to scoop the flesh into the bowl of a food processor. Add the zest of the 2 limes and the remaining juice of 1 lime to the food processor. Add the red wine vinegar and some salt. With the machine running, stream in the remaining 3 tablespoons of EVOO and a couple of shakes of hot sauce. Stop the processor, taste the dressing, and adjust the seasonings with more salt, pepper, and hot sauce to taste.

Wipe out the skillet you cooked the halibut in. Place it over high heat and blister the tortillas in the dry pan for a few seconds on each side. As you remove them from the pan have a clean kitchen towel handy to wrap them in and help keep them warm and soft. You can also simply wrap the tortillas in a barely damp kitchen towel and heat them in the microwave until they are warm and supple.

To assemble, arrange a pile of the halibut-corn-romaine mixture on a warm tortilla, top it with a spoonful of the avocado dressing, wrap, and roll it up. Eat and enjoy.

EXPRESS LANE SHOPPING LIST

- ❑ 4 fresh halibut steaks or fillets, 6 to 8 ounces each
- ❑ 1 jalapeño pepper
- ❑ 1 romaine heart
- ❑ 1 bunch fresh cilantro
- ❑ 2 ripe Hass avocados
- ❑ 1 package 6-inch soft flour tortillas

And make sure you have the following On Hand:

EVOO • Chili powder • Limes • Salt • Onion • Garlic • Black pepper • Frozen corn kernels • Chicken stock • Red wine vinegar • Hot sauce (optional)

Spanish-Style Chicken with Mushroom-Chorizo Sauce and Butter-Herb Spani-Spuds

This is a real-deal, square meal (that is, one you might find in a restaurant on a square in Barcelona!).

4 SERVINGS

- 2 pounds **boiling potatoes**
- 3 tablespoons chopped or snipped **chives**, about 10
- 2 tablespoons cold **butter**, cut into pieces
- ½ cup fresh **flat-leaf parsley**, a couple of handfuls, chopped
  Salt and **black pepper**
  A few shakes of **hot sauce**, such as Tabasco
- ¼ cup **EVOO** (extra-virgin olive oil)
- 4 boneless, skinless **chicken breasts**
- 1 teaspoon **dried thyme**, ⅓ palmful
- 2 teaspoons **paprika**, ⅔ palmful
- ½ pound **chorizo** sausage, cut into quarters lengthwise, then finely chopped
- ½ pound **button mushrooms**, stemmed and thinly sliced
- 2 **portobello mushroom caps**, thinly sliced
- ½ pound **shiitake, oyster, or cremini mushrooms**, or whichever funky mushrooms your store carries, stemmed and thinly sliced
- 1 medium yellow **onion**, chopped
- 4 large **garlic cloves**, chopped
- ½ cup **dry sherry**, a couple of glugs
- 1 cup **chicken stock**

> **TIDBIT**
> Sherry is a great thing to have on hand in the wine rack. You can use it in Marsalas, dressings, soups, or any chicken dish. One of my favorite appetizers is mushrooms cooked in garlic, butter, and sherry.

Put the potatoes in a saucepot, cover them with water, and place the pot over high heat to bring them to a boil. Cook them for about 12 minutes, or until they are fork tender. Once cooked, drain the potatoes and return them to the pot, then place them over medium heat for about 1 minute to dry them out a bit. Turn the heat off and add the chives, butter, half of the parsley, salt, pepper, and hot sauce to taste. Stir the potatoes until the butter has melted, then transfer to a serving platter.

While the potatoes are cooking, preheat a large skillet over medium-high heat with 2 tablespoons of the EVOO, twice around the pan. Season the chicken with salt, pepper, the thyme, and the paprika. Add the chicken to the skillet and cook it on each side for 5 to 6 minutes, or until it is cooked through. Remove the chicken from the skillet to a plate and cover it loosely with foil to keep it warm. Return the skillet to the cooktop over medium-high heat. Add the remaining 2 table-spoons of EVOO and the chorizo and cook, stirring it frequently, for about 2 minutes. Remove the chorizo from the skillet to a plate using a slotted spoon and reserve.

Turn the heat up to high and add the mushrooms to the skillet. Spread them out in an even layer and resist the temptation to stir for a couple of minutes so that the mushrooms can start to brown. Once they are brown, go ahead and shake the pan up, stir, and continue to cook them for 2 minutes more, then add the onions, garlic, and reserved chorizo and sea-son with salt and pepper. Continue to cook, stirring every now and then, for about 3 minutes, or until the onions start to look tender. Add the sherry and cook for 1 minute more, then add the chicken stock and bring it up to a bubble. Simmer for about 2 minutes. Add the remaining pars-ley and stir it to combine, then taste and adjust the seasonings with salt and pepper.

To serve, arrange the cooked chicken breasts on serving plates, top with the mushroom-chorizo sauce, and serve the butter and herb spuds alongside.

Black Pepper and Coriander–Crusted Tuna with Orange and Fennel–Roasted Potato Salad

Here's a hipster menu for urbanites or just hep hicks from the sticks like me.

4 SERVINGS

- 2 pounds red or white **boiling potatoes**, washed
- 8 tablespoons **EVOO** (extra-virgin olive oil)
- 1 tablespoon **grill seasoning** such as McCormick's Montreal Steak Seasoning, a palmful
- 1 **fennel bulb**, fronds trimmed and chopped, the bulb quartered, core removed and discarded, quarters thinly sliced lengthwise
- ½ small **red onion**, thinly sliced
- 10 fresh **basil leaves**, chopped, about ½ cup
- ¼ cup fresh **flat-leaf parsley**, a generous handful, chopped

  Zest and juice of 1 orange

- 1 tablespoon **Dijon mustard** (eyeball it)

  Salt and **black pepper**

- ¼ cup **all-purpose flour**
- 1 tablespoon **ground coriander**, a palmful
- 1 tablespoon **coarse black pepper**, a palmful
- 4 1½-inch-thick **tuna steaks**

EXPRESS LANE
SHOPPING LIST

❑ 1 fennel bulb

❑ 1 small red onion

❑ 1 bunch fresh basil

❑ 1 orange

❑ 4 1½-inch-thick tuna
   steaks, 6 ounces each

Preheat the oven to 450°F.

Cut the potatoes into wedges and drop them onto a cookie sheet. Coat the potatoes in 3 tablespoons of the EVOO. Season the spuds with the grill seasoning. Roast the potatoes, turning them once, for 25 minutes, until tender and brown at the edges and a bit crusty.

In a large salad bowl, combine the fennel fronds, thinly sliced fennel, red onion, basil, and parsley. In a small bowl, combine the orange zest and juice with the Dijon mustard and a little salt and pepper. In a slow steady stream, whisk in 3 tablespoons of the EVOO. Pour the dressing over the fennel salad, toss to coat, and reserve.

When the potatoes have about 10 more minutes to roast, start the tuna. In a shallow dish, combine the flour, coriander, and coarsely ground black pepper and a little salt. Pat the tuna steaks dry and then coat them in the flour mixture, pressing it in lightly. Preheat a large nonstick skillet over high heat with the remaining 2 tablespoons of EVOO, twice around the pan. When the pan is very hot, add the steaks. Sear and brown the tuna steaks for 2 minutes, then turn, and immediately reduce the heat to medium. Loosely tent the pan with aluminum foil and cook the steaks 5 minutes for rare, 7 minutes for medium. The steaks should be firm but have a little give, and some pink should remain at the center.

Remove the roasted potatoes from the oven and add them to the dressed fennel salad, tossing to combine. Taste them for seasoning and add a little salt and pepper if you want. Serve the tuna steaks alongside the orange and fennel–roasted potato salad.

And make sure you have the following On Hand:

Red or white boiling potatoes • EVOO • Grill seasoning • Flat-leaf parsley • Dijon mustard • Salt and black pepper • Flour • Ground coriander • Coarse black pepper

Chunky Chicken and Corn Chili with Spicy Citrus Salsa over Rice

I'm always trying to come up with yet another version of chili and yet another chicken dinner. Here's both in one meal in *another* new way.

4 SERVINGS

- 3 tablespoons **vegetable oil**, plus more for drizzling
- 1½ cups **white rice**

  Salt and **black pepper**
- 5½ cups **chicken stock**
- 2 pounds **chicken tenders**, cut into bite-size pieces
- 1 large **onion**, chopped
- 4 large **garlic cloves**, chopped
- 1 **jalapeño pepper**, seeded and finely chopped
- 1 red **bell pepper**, chopped
- 1½ tablespoons **chili powder**, 1½ palmfuls
- ½ tablespoon **ground cumin**, ½ palmful
- 2 tablespoons **all-purpose flour**
- 1 10-ounce box **frozen corn kernels**
- 2 **oranges**

  Zest and juice of 1 lime
- ¼ cup fresh **cilantro leaves**, a generous handful, coarsely chopped
- ½ cup fresh **flat-leaf parsley**, a couple of handfuls, coarsely chopped

  Hot sauce, to taste (optional)

To make the rice, heat a medium pot with a tight-fitting lid over medium-high heat. Add 1 tablespoon of the vegetable oil, once around the pan, then add the rice; stir to coat the rice in the oil and toast lightly, for about 1 minute. Season with salt and pepper, then add 2½ cups of the chicken stock and bring up to a bubble. Cover the pot, reduce the heat to a simmer, and cook for 15 to 18 minutes, until the rice is tender.

To make the chili, preheat a medium soup pot over medium-high heat with the remaining 2 tablespoons of oil. Add the chunked up chicken pieces and season with salt and pepper. Brown the chicken on all sides for about 3 to 4 minutes. Remove the chicken from the pot to a plate and reserve. Add a little drizzle of oil to the pot and add the onions, garlic, three fourths of the chopped jalapeño, and the bell peppers. Season with the chili powder, cumin, salt, and pepper and cook for about 3 minutes, stirring frequently. Dust the vegetables liberally with the flour and continue to cook for 1 minute. Stir in the remaining 3 cups of chicken stock to the vegetables, bring up to a bubble, and then stir in the corn and add the chicken back to the pot. Turn the heat down to medium low and simmer gently for 10 minutes.

While the chili is simmering, make the spicy citrus salsa. With a paring knife, cut the peel and pith from the oranges. Cut the peeled oranges into disks and then cut the disks into quarters. Toss the oranges in a small mixing bowl with the remaining jalapeño, the lime zest, a little salt and pepper, and about 1 tablespoon of the chopped cilantro. Stir to combine.

Once the chili has simmered for 10 minutes, turn off the heat and add the lime juice, the remaining cilantro, and the chopped parsley. Taste and check for seasoning and add more salt and pepper if needed. If you want a little more heat, throw in a couple dashes of hot sauce.

Fluff the tender rice with a fork and then divide it among 4 serving bowls. Top each portion of rice with some of the chili and garnish with a heaping spoonful of the spicy citrus salsa.

EXPRESS LANE SHOPPING LIST

☐ **2 pounds** chicken tenders
☐ **1** jalapeño pepper
☐ **1 red** bell pepper
☐ **2** oranges
☐ **1 bunch** fresh cilantro

And make sure you have the following On Hand:

Vegetable oil • White rice • Salt and black pepper • Chicken stock • Onion • Garlic • Chili powder • Ground cumin • Flour • Frozen corn kernels • Lime • Flat-leaf parsley • Hot sauce (optional)

Steaks with Tangy Corn Relish and Super Cheese and Scallion Smashed Spuds

This is a gut bustingly delicious twist on steak and bakers.

4 SERVINGS

2 to 2¼ pounds red or white **boiling potatoes** (if larger than a golf ball, cut them in half)

4 tablespoons **EVOO** (extra-virgin olive oil)

2 medium **onions**, thinly sliced

4 **garlic cloves**, chopped

1½ tablespoons **chili powder**, 1½ palmfuls

1 teaspoon **ground cumin**, ⅓ palmful

1 tablespoon **sugar**

Salt and **black pepper**

4 1-inch-thick **Delmonico steaks**

Grill seasoning, such as McCormick's Montreal Steak Seasoning, to taste

1½ cups **chicken stock**

1 10-ounce box **frozen corn kernels**

2 ounces **cream cheese**, at room temperature

2 cups shredded **Cheddar cheese**

4 **scallions**, thinly sliced

2 **limes**, both zested, one juiced, the other cut into quarters

¼ cup fresh **cilantro leaves**, a generous handful, coarsely chopped

Place the potatoes in a medium-size sauce pot, add enough water to cover them by an inch or two, and place over high heat to bring it up to a boil. Boil the potatoes for about 12 minutes, or until they are fork tender.

To start the corn relish, preheat a medium-size skillet over medium-high heat with 2 tablespoons of the EVOO, twice around the pan. Add the onions, garlic, chili powder, cumin, sugar, salt, and pepper. Cook for 4 to 5 minutes, stirring frequently, until the onions start to take on a golden color and are nice and tender.

While the onions for the corn relish are cooking, preheat a large skillet over medium-high heat with the remaining 2 tablespoons of EVOO. Pat the steaks dry with a paper towel, and season liberally with the grill seasoning. Add the steaks to the hot skillet and cook on each side for 4 to 5 minutes for rare; 5 to 6 minutes for medium. Remove them from the skillet and let the steaks rest, loosely covered with foil, for about 5 minutes.

Once you have the steaks going, get back to the corn relish. Add the chicken stock and bring the liquid up to a bubble. Add the corn and continue to cook for about 2 to 3 minutes, or until the liquids have reduced by half.

Check on the boiling potatoes. If tender, drain and return them to the hot pot. Smash the potatoes with a masher and combine them with the cream cheese, Cheddar cheese, and scallions. Season with a little salt and pepper. Resmash, taste, and adjust the seasonings.

To the corn relish add the lime zest and juice and the cilantro. Stir to combine and taste the relish to adjust the seasoning with salt and pepper.

Squeeze a quarter of a lime over each of the rested steaks. Serve the steaks with a large helping of the tangy corn relish and a big mound of the super smashed spuds.

EXPRESS LANE SHOPPING LIST

- ❑ 4 1-inch-thick Delmonico steaks, 8 to 10 ounces each
- ❑ 4-ounce package cream cheese
- ❑ 1 10-ounce sack shredded Cheddar cheese
- ❑ 1 bunch scallions
- ❑ 1 bunch fresh cilantro

And make sure you have the following On Hand:

Red or white boiling potatoes • EVOO • Onions • Garlic • Chili powder • Ground cumin • Sugar • Salt and black pepper • Grill seasoning • Chicken stock • Frozen corn kernels • Limes

Chicken with Roasted Red Pepper, Chorizo, and Sweet Pea Sauce over Rice

This is my chicken and rice recipe number 14,654. But, *this* one is as colorful as it is flavorful!

4 SERVINGS

- 3 tablespoons **EVOO** (extra-virgin olive oil)
- 1 tablespoon **butter**
- 1 large **onion**, chopped
- **Salt** and **black pepper**
- 1½ cups **white rice**
- 3 cups **chicken stock**
- 4 boneless, skinless **chicken breasts**
- ½ tablespoon **smoked sweet paprika**, ½ palmful
- 1 teaspoon **dried thyme**, ⅓ palmful
- ¾ pound **chorizo**, halved lengthwise, then thinly sliced
- 2 large **garlic cloves**, chopped
- ½ small **carrot**, peeled and grated
- 2 **jarred roasted red peppers**, chopped
- 1 10-ounce box **frozen peas**
- ¼ cup fresh **flat-leaf parsley**, a generous handful, chopped

Heat a medium-size sauce pot with a tight-fitting lid over medium heat with 1 tablespoon of the EVOO, once around the pan, and the butter. Add one fourth of the chopped onion, season with salt and pepper, and cook for about 1 minute. Add the rice and stir to coat in the oil. Add 2½ cups of the chicken stock to the

EXPRESS LANE
SHOPPING LIST

❑ 4 boneless, skinless
   chicken breasts,
   6 ounces each
❑ ¾ pound chorizo

rice and bring it up to a simmer. Cover the pot with the lid and turn the heat down to medium low. Cook the rice for 15 to 18 minutes, or until it is tender and cooked through.

While the rice is cooking, start the chicken. Preheat a large skillet over medium-high heat with the remaining 2 tablespoons of oil. Season the chicken breasts with the paprika, salt, pepper, and the thyme; add the seasoned chicken to the skillet. Cook the breasts for 5 to 6 minutes on each side, or until cooked through.

Remove the chicken from the skillet to a plate and loosely cover it with aluminum foil. Return the skillet to the cooktop over medium-high heat and add the chorizo. Cook for 2 minutes, stirring frequently. Add the remaining chopped onion, the garlic, carrot, and roasted red peppers to the chorizo and season it with a little salt and pepper. Cook until the onions are slightly tender, about 2 to 3 minutes. Add the remaining ½ cup of chicken stock, and scrape up any bits that have stuck to the bottom of the pan. Add the frozen peas and parsley; continue to cook for 1 to 2 minutes to heat the peas through. Taste and adjust the seasonings with a little salt and pepper.

To serve, arrange the chicken breasts on dinner plates and top them with lots of sauce. Fluff the rice with a fork and serve alongside.

And make sure you have the following On Hand:

EVOO • Butter • Onion • Salt and black pepper • White rice • Chicken stock • Smoked paprika • Dried thyme • Garlic • Carrot • Jarred roasted red peppers • Frozen peas • Flat-leaf parsley

Broiled Lamb Chops with Mediterranean Potato-Veggie Mix

Lamb chops are always perfect for 30MM because they are quick cooking. If you are the type who only indulges in leg of lamb once a year at holidays, pick up some chops and try this one at home tonight.

4 SERVINGS

- 4 tablespoons **EVOO** (extra-virgin olive oil)
- 1 large **baking potato**, scrubbed clean
- **Salt** and **black pepper**
- ¼ teaspoon **dried thyme** (eyeball it)
- 1 large **fennel bulb**, cut in quarters, cored, and thinly sliced, a few fronds reserved
- 1 large **onion**, thinly sliced
- 3 large **garlic cloves**, chopped
- ¼ teaspoon **red pepper flakes** (eyeball it)
- 1½ cups **chicken stock**
- 2 pounds **rack of lamb**, cut into individual chops, 3 to 4 chops per person
- 1 tablespoon **balsamic vinegar** (eyeball it)
- 10 **kalamata olives**, pitted and coarsely chopped, ½ cup
- 10 fresh **mint leaves**, a few sprigs, chopped
- ¾ cup fresh **basil**, 15 leaves, chopped

Preheat the broiler to high. Place the rack about 6 inches from the heat.

Preheat a large nonstick skillet over medium-high heat with 2 tablespoons of the EVOO, twice around the pan. Quarter the potato lengthwise, then thinly slice it across into small, thin bite-size pieces. Add the potatoes to the hot skillet and spread them out in an even layer across the pan. Season the potatoes with salt, pepper, and thyme. Resist the temptation to shake or stir the pan for a few minutes, until the potatoes start to brown up. Once they are a little brown on the first side, turn them and continue to cook them until they are evenly golden and cooked through, about 8 to 10 minutes. Turn the heat down a little if the potatoes start browning faster than they are cooking through.

While the potatoes are working, preheat a second skillet over medium-high heat with the remaining 2 tablespoons of EVOO. Add the sliced fennel, onions, garlic, red pepper flakes, salt, and pepper. Cook until both the onions and the fennel are tender, about 4 to 5 minutes, stirring frequently. Add the chicken stock and bring up to a bubble, then simmer for 3 minutes or until there is very little liquid left in the pan, less than $\frac{1}{2}$ cup.

Arrange the chops on a broiler pan. Season both sides of the lamb chops with salt and pepper and broil them for 4 minutes on each side for medium rare.

Add the balsamic vinegar and olives to the skillet with the fennel, tossing to combine them. Turn the heat down to low while the chops finish broiling. Once the chops are ready to come out of the broiler, add the mint and basil to the fennel, add the cooked browned-up potatoes, and toss to combine. Serve the chops alongside the fennel and potatoes and garnish with the fennel fronds.

EXPRESS LANE SHOPPING LIST

- ☐ 1 large fennel bulb
- ☐ 2 small racks of lamb
- ☐ 10 kalamata olives, about a ½ cup
- ☐ 1 bunch fresh mint
- ☐ 1 bunch fresh basil

And make sure you have the following On Hand:

EVOO • Baking potato • Salt and black pepper • Dried thyme • Onion • Garlic • Red pepper flakes • Chicken stock • Balsamic vinegar

Chicken with Apple-Mushroom Sauce and Steamed Asparagus

Chicken and applesauce . . . sounds like hospital food, huh? Well, if that were the only way to get this elegant, savory supper, I'd check *myself* in!

4 SERVINGS

- 2 tablespoons **EVOO** (extra-virgin olive oil), twice around the pan
- 4 boneless, skinless **chicken breasts**

  Salt and **black pepper**
- 1 teaspoon **dried thyme**, 1/3 palmful
- 1 teaspoon **poultry seasoning**, 1/3 palmful
- 1 pound pencil-thin **asparagus**, tough ends trimmed

  Juice of 1/2 lemon
- 2 tablespoons **butter**
- 8 **button mushrooms**, thinly sliced
- 2 **shallots**, finely chopped
- 1 small **green apple**, peeled, cored, and thinly sliced
- 1 shot of **Calvados** or other apple brandy (look for a nip, a 2-ounce bottle; see Note)
- 1 cup **chicken stock**, plus more as needed to thin out the sauce
- 1/4 cup **sour cream**
- 2 tablespoons chopped fresh **flat-leaf parsley**, a palmful

> **NOTE:** If you cannot find Calvados in a nip size and you're not into buying an entire bottle, don't sweat it! Calvados is just apple brandy, so you can get close to that flavor by substituting about 1/4 cup of apple cider or juice, 1 teaspoon of sugar, and a big splash of white wine.

Preheat a large skillet over medium-high heat with the EVOO. Season the chicken breasts with salt, pepper, the thyme, and the poultry seasoning and add them to the skillet. Cook the chicken on each side for 5 to 6 minutes, or until it is cooked through.

While the chicken is cooking, fill a medium skillet with about ½ inch of water. Place the skillet over high heat; cover it to bring it up to a boil quickly. Once boiling, add salt and the trimmed asparagus. If you have pencil-thin asparagus about 2 minutes will do the trick; if you have thicker asparagus cook for 3 to 4 minutes. You want them to be tender but remain green. Once cooked, drain the asparagus and return them to the skillet; season with salt, pepper, and the lemon juice. Shake the pan to spread the seasoning over the asparagus.

Remove the chicken from the skillet to a plate and loosely cover it with aluminum foil. Return the skillet to the heat and add the butter; once melted, add the sliced mushrooms and season with black pepper. Cook the mushrooms until lightly browned, 3 to 4 minutes, stirring occasionally. Add the shallots and the sliced apples and season with salt. Continue to cook for another couple of minutes. Add the Calvados and cook a minute more. Add the chicken stock, bring up to a bubble, and simmer for 3 to 4 minutes. Add the sour cream and parsley, stir to incorporate, and heat through, 1 minute. If the sauce is too thick for your liking, add another splash of chicken stock.

Arrange the chicken breasts on serving plates, spoon some sauce with a portion of the apples and mushrooms over the top, and serve the asparagus tips alongside.

Double-Dipped Buttermilk Chicken Fingers on Spinach Salad with Blue Cheese Dressing

You have to buy a quart of buttermilk in order to get the 2 cups you need for this recipe, but I've got your back on the extra 2 cups: transfer it to a large resealable food storage bag and freeze it. Don't forget to label the bag—if you're like me, you have enough mystery items in your freezer already! Use the buttermilk to make this recipe again, or check out the recipe for Bacon and Creamy Ranch Chicken Burgers with Crispy Scallion "Sticks" on page 236.

4 SERVINGS

Zest and juice of 2 **lemons**

A few dashes of **hot sauce**

1 cup **blue cheese crumbles**

½ cup **sour cream**

1 **celery rib**, finely chopped

Salt and **black pepper**

Vegetable oil, for frying

3 cups **all-purpose flour** (eyeball it—I scoop mine out with a coffee cup)

2 cups **buttermilk**

1 teaspoon **paprika**, ⅓ palmful

1½ to 2 pounds **chicken tenders**

1 pound triple-washed **spinach**, stemmed and chopped

½ small **red onion**, thinly sliced

10 **button mushrooms**, stemmed and thinly sliced

In a small mixing bowl, combine the lemon juice, hot sauce, crumbled blue cheese, sour cream, celery, salt, and pepper. Mix the dressing well and reserve.

Preheat $1\frac{1}{2}$ inches of vegetable oil in a large deep skillet. While the oil is heating, set up a breading assembly line near the stove. Put the flour in a large, wide bowl; pour the buttermilk into a second large, wide bowl; then stir in the lemon zest and paprika. Season the chicken tenders with salt and pepper. Working in 2 or 3 batches, dust the chicken tenders in the flour, shake off the excess, then coat in the buttermilk. Transfer them back to the flour and coat them thoroughly, then back to the buttermilk, and then back into the flour for one last coating.

To test the oil temperature, add a 1-inch cube of bread to the hot oil. If it turns deep golden brown by a count of 40, the oil is ready. If the bread cube browns too quickly, turn down the heat and wait a few minutes for it to cool down. Carefully place the first batch of coated tenders in the hot oil. Fry the tenders in small batches for 6 to 7 minutes, turning when the first side has become golden brown. Once cooked, remove from the oil to a paper-towel-lined plate and immediately sprinkle them with a little salt. Repeat until all the tenders are fried.

After the last batch of tenders goes into the oil, combine the spinach, red onion, and sliced mushrooms in a large salad bowl. Pour half of the dressing over the salad and toss it to coat. Top the salad with the fried chicken tenders, whole or chopped, your choice, and serve the remaining dressing on the side for dipping.

EXPRESS LANE SHOPPING LIST

- ❏ **3 or 4 ounce package** blue cheese crumbles
- ❏ **1 8-ounce container** sour cream
- ❏ **1 quart** buttermilk
- ❏ **1½ to 2 pounds** chicken tenders, **2 small packs or one family-size pack**
- ❏ **1 pound triple-washed** spinach
- ❏ **1 small** red onion
- ❏ **10 button mushrooms**

And make sure you have the following On Hand:

Lemons • Hot sauce • Celery • Salt and black pepper • Vegetable oil • Flour • Paprika

French Onion Soup with an Italian Attitude

The French are notorious for their stuffy and particular attitudes . . . especially when it comes to food, but they've got nothing on the Sicilians. It takes a Sicilian 'tude to think one could improve on a French classic, especially in 30 minutes. Well, *this* Sicilian says "Bring it on."

4 SERVINGS

- 1 tablespoon **EVOO** (extra-virgin olive oil), once around the pan
- 2 tablespoons **butter**
- 6 medium **onions**, thinly sliced

  Salt and **black pepper**

  Leaves from 1 sprig of **rosemary**, finely chopped
- ½ pint **grape tomatoes**, halved
- ½ cup fresh **basil**, about 10 leaves
- ¼ cup shredded or grated **Parmigiano-Reggiano** cheese, a handful
- 4 thick slices **crusty bread**
- 1 **garlic clove**, crushed
- 1 tablespoon **balsamic vinegar** (eyeball it)
- ½ cup **white wine**, a couple of good glugs
- 6 cups **beef stock**
- 8 slices fresh **mozzarella** cheese

EXPRESS LANE
SHOPPING LIST

❑ **Fresh** rosemary **sprig**

❑ **1 pint** grape tomatoes

❑ **1 bunch fresh** basil

❑ **1 ball** fresh mozzarella

❑ **1 loaf** crusty bread

Preheat the broiler to high.

Heat a deep pot over medium to medium-high heat. Add the EVOO and butter to the pot. When the butter melts, start adding the onions as you slice them. Season the onions with salt, pepper, and the rosemary. Cook the onions for 15 to 18 minutes, until tender, sweet, and caramel colored, stirring frequently. If you find that the onions are burning in spots before browning all over, add a splash of water and stir now and then, scraping the bottom of the pot.

And make sure you have
the following On Hand:

EVOO • Butter • Onions •
Salt and black pepper •
Parmigiano-Reggiano cheese
• Garlic • Balsamic vinegar
• White wine • Beef stock

While the onions are cooking, make the topping. In a small bowl, combine the grape tomatoes, basil, grated cheese, salt, and pepper. Under the broiler or toaster oven, toast the crusty bread until golden; rub each side of the golden toast with the crushed garlic clove.

Once the onions are done, add the balsamic vinegar and white wine, stirring up all the brown bits from the bottom of the pot. Add the stock and cover the pot to bring the soup up to a quick boil.

Arrange 4 small, deep soup bowls or crocks on a cookie sheet. Once the soup reaches a boil, ladle it into the bowls. Float a toasted bread slice on each serving and cover each toast with a mound of the grape tomato mixture. Top with 2 slices of the mozzarella cheese. Slide the cookie sheet under the hot broiler until the cheese melts and bubbles.

Grilled Chicken Pasta Salad

Talk about flexible, this chicken is a cheerleader. Yes, it's equally good steaming hot or icebox cold. Eat this dish four seasons of the year, hot or not, indoors or out. It's G-R-E-A-T . . . *great*!

4 SERVINGS

Salt

½ pound **short-cut pasta**

3 **garlic cloves**, chopped

2 tablespoons **grill seasoning**, such as McCormick's Montreal Steak Seasoning, 2 palmfuls

2 teaspoons **hot sauce** (eyeball it)

3 tablespoons **Worcestershire sauce** (eyeball it)

5 tablespoons **red wine vinegar**

½ cup **EVOO** (extra-virgin olive oil; eyeball it)

2 large **onions**, sliced 1 inch thick

6 thin-cut **chicken breast cutlets**

2 tablespoons **Dijon mustard** (eyeball it)

Black pepper

¼ cup grated **Parmigiano-Reggiano** or Pecorino Romano cheese, a handful

2 bunches **arugula**, thoroughly washed and coarsely chopped

1 small head **radicchio**, cored and coarsely chopped

2 cups fresh **basil**, 20 leaves, coarsely chopped

¼ cup fresh **flat-leaf parsley**, a generous handful, chopped

3 **celery ribs**, thinly sliced

1 ball **fresh mozzarella** cheese, cut into bite-size pieces

1 pint **grape tomatoes**, left whole if small, cut in half if large

Heat a grill pan or outdoor grill to high heat.

Bring a large pot of water with a tight-fitting lid to a boil over high heat. Once the water boils, add some salt and the pasta, and cook according to package directions until al dente.

In a small bowl, mix the garlic, grill seasoning, hot sauce, Worcestershire sauce, and 2 tablespoons of the vinegar. Whisk in ¼ cup of the EVOO. Divide the mixture between two shallow bowls. Add the sliced onions to one and the chicken cutlets to the other. Toss to coat both thoroughly and marinate for a few minutes.

In a salad bowl, combine the mustard and the remaining 3 tablespoons of vinegar with a little salt and pepper. In a slow, steady stream, whisk in the remaining ¼ cup of EVOO, then add the grated cheese. Once the pasta is cooked, drain it thoroughly and add it to the salad bowl with the dressing; toss to coat. Since you are adding the pasta while it is still hot, the dressing will really soak into the pasta.

Grill the onion slices, cooking them on each side until well marked, about 2 to 3 minutes. Grill the chicken cutlets for 3 to 4 minutes on each side. Remove the onions and the chicken from the grill to a cutting board to rest and cool off for about 5 minutes. Coarsely chop the grilled onions and cut the chicken into thin strips. Add them to the dressed pasta. Add the arugula, radicchio, basil, parsley, celery, mozzarella, and grape tomatoes. Season with a little salt and pepper and toss thoroughly.

EXPRESS LANE SHOPPING LIST

- ❑ **6 thin-cut** chicken breast cutlets
- ❑ **2 bunches** arugula
- ❑ **1 small head** radicchio
- ❑ **1 bunch fresh** basil
- ❑ **1 ball** fresh mozzarella
- ❑ **1 pint** grape tomatoes

And make sure you have the following On Hand:

Salt • Short-cut pasta • Garlic • Grill seasoning • Hot sauce • Worcestershire • Red wine vinegar • EVOO • Onions • Dijon mustard • Black pepper • Parmigiano-Reggiano or Pecorino Romano cheese • Flat-leaf parsley • Celery

Messy Giuseppe

Italian-style Sloppy Joes—get it? Hah! I kill me! Funny! Well, I thought so, anyway . . .

4 SERVINGS

2 tablespoons **EVOO** (extra-virgin olive oil), twice around the pan

½ teaspoon **red pepper flakes**

1 pound **ground sirloin**, 90 percent lean

1 **green bell pepper**, cored, seeded, and chopped

1 small **onion**, chopped

5 large **garlic cloves**, chopped

¼ teaspoon freshly grated **nutmeg** (eyeball it)

Coarse salt and **black pepper**

1 medium **portobello mushroom cap**, finely chopped

½ cup **red wine**, a couple of glugs

¾ cup **beef stock**

1 14-ounce can **crushed tomatoes**

¼ cup fresh **flat-leaf parsley**, a generous handful, chopped

6 tablespoons (¾ stick) **butter**, super soft

1 cup fresh **basil**, about 10 leaves, chopped

4 individual **ciabatta rolls** or hoagie rolls

½ cup grated **Parmigiano-Reggiano** or Pecorino Romano cheese, a few handfuls

1 ball **fresh mozzarella** cheese, cut into 8 slices

Preheat the broiler to high.

To make the meat sauce, heat a deep skillet or a heavy-bottomed pot over medium-high heat. Add the EVOO, red pepper flakes, and ground beef, and break up the meat. Add the green pepper, onions, three fourths of the garlic, the nutmeg, and a little salt and pepper to the beef and cook together, using the back of a wooden spoon to break the meat into tiny bits as it browns. Add the mushrooms and cook for 5 minutes more. Add the wine and cook for 1 minute, then add the beef stock and tomatoes. Bring the mixture up to a bubble, reduce the heat to medium low, and gently simmer for 10 minutes. Finish it by stirring in the chopped parsley.

While the meat is simmering, combine the remaining garlic with the soft butter, chopped basil, and a little salt and pepper. Split the rolls in half lengthwise without separating the halves. Press open the rolls, flattening them out a little bit. Slather the insides with the garlic butter and toast until golden brown under the broiler.

Top one side of the garlicky, toasted rolls with a heap of meat, sprinkle each pile of meat sauce with some grated cheese, and top that with 2 slices of the mozzarella. Transfer them to the broiler to melt the cheese. Remove them from the broiler and prepare to get sloppy with Messy Giuseppe!

EXPRESS LANE SHOPPING LIST

- ❑ **1 pound** ground sirloin, **90 percent lean**
- ❑ **1 green** bell pepper
- ❑ **1 medium** portobello mushroom cap
- ❑ **1 bunch fresh** basil
- ❑ **4 individual** ciabatta rolls **or other crusty hoagie rolls**
- ❑ **1 ball** fresh mozzarella

And make sure you have the following On Hand:

EVOO • Red pepper flakes • Onion • Garlic • Nutmeg • Coarse salt and black pepper • Red wine • Beef stock • Canned crushed tomatoes • Flat-leaf parsley • Butter • Parmigiano-Reggiano or Pecorino Romano cheese

Sautéed Chicken with Rosemary, Olive, and Roasted Pepper Sauce over Orange Rice

For *me,* this is chicken and rice recipe number 14,655. And for you?

4 SERVINGS

- 3 tablespoons EVOO (extra-virgin olive oil)
- Zest and juice of 1 orange
- ¼ cup golden raisins, a generous handful
- 1½ cups white rice
- 1 bay leaf
- Salt and black pepper
- 3½ cups chicken stock
- 5 bacon slices, coarsely chopped
- 2 sprigs fresh rosemary, leaves finely chopped
- 4 boneless, skinless chicken breasts
- 1 large onion, thinly sliced
- 2 celery ribs, finely chopped
- 3 large garlic cloves, chopped
- 1 teaspoon dried thyme, ⅓ palmful
- ½ teaspoon red pepper flakes
- ½ cup white wine, a couple of glugs
- 12 big Sicilian green olives, pitted and halved
- 2 jarred roasted red peppers, coarsely chopped
- ¼ cup fresh flat-leaf parsley, a generous handful, chopped

❑ 1 orange

❑ 1 2-ounce box golden
   raisins

❑ Fresh rosemary,
   2 sprigs

❑ 4 boneless, skinless
   chicken breasts,
   6 to 8 ounces each

❑ 12 big Sicilian green olives

Heat a medium pot with a tight-fitting lid over medium-high heat. Add 1 tablespoon of the EVOO, once around the pan. Add the orange zest, raisins, rice, bay leaf, salt, and pepper and stir them to coat in the oil. Add $2\frac{1}{2}$ cups of the chicken stock. Bring the stock to a boil, cover the pot, and reduce the heat to a simmer. Cook for 15 to 18 minutes, until the rice is tender. Discard the bay leaf.

Heat a large skillet over medium-high heat with the remaining 2 tablespoons of EVOO. Add the bacon and cook it until it's nice and crispy, about 2 to 3 minutes.

In a shallow dish, combine the juice of $\frac{1}{2}$ orange, half of the rosemary, and salt and pepper. Add the chicken and turn to coat.

Remove the crisp bacon from the skillet to a paper-towel-lined plate and reserve. Return the skillet to the heat and add the seasoned chicken breasts. Cook the chicken for 5 to 6 minutes on each side, or until cooked through. Remove the chicken to a plate and cover it loosely with foil. Return the skillet to the heat and add the onions, celery, garlic, thyme, red pepper flakes, salt, pepper, and the remaining rosemary. Cook for about 3 minutes, stirring frequently, until the onions are slightly tender. Add the juice of half an orange and the wine, cook for a minute, then add the remaining cup of chicken stock and the green olives and bring up to a bubble. Return the chicken to the skillet and cook for 3 more minutes. Add the roasted red peppers, parsley, and reserved crispy bacon; stir to incorporate.

Serve the chicken and sauce over the rice.

And make sure you have the following On Hand:

EVOO • White rice • Bay leaf • Salt and black pepper • Chicken stock • Bacon • Onion • Celery • Garlic • Dried thyme • Red pepper flakes • White wine • Jarred roasted red peppers • Flat-leaf parsley

Spicy Black Bean Soup with Limed-Up Shrimp

Rich, but not heavy, this dish is delish.

4 SERVINGS

 5 tablespoons **EVOO** (extra-virgin olive oil)
 1 medium **onion**, finely chopped
 4 **garlic cloves**, chopped
 2 tablespoons **chili powder**, 2 palmfuls
 1 teaspoon **ground cumin**, ⅓ palmful
   Salt and **black pepper**
 ½ teaspoon **red pepper flakes**
   Zest and juice of 2 limes
 ¼ cup fresh **flat-leaf parsley**, a generous handful, chopped
 16 **jumbo shrimp**, peeled, deveined, and butterflied (see Note)
 2 14-ounce cans **black beans**, rinsed and drained
 1 14-ounce can diced **fire-roasted tomatoes**
 5 cups **chicken stock**
 ½ cup **heavy cream** (optional)
   Hot sauce, to taste

> NOTE: Cut along the shrimp where it has been deveined, separating it without cutting all the way through it. Press it open a bit, or "butterfly" it. When the shrimp cook, they will continue to open and curl, allowing you to arrange them literally standing up in the soup. If you prefer to serve the shrimp on the side, skip the butterfly process.

Heat a medium soup pot over medium-high heat with 2 tablespoons of the EVOO, twice around the pan. Add the onions, three fourths of the garlic, the chili powder, cumin, salt, and pepper. Cook for about 3 to 4 minutes or until the onions are tender, stirring frequently.

While the onions are cooking, in a shallow dish combine the remaining garlic, the remaining 3 tablespoons of EVOO, the red pepper flakes, lime zest, parsley, and a little salt. Add the shrimp and coat them thoroughly in the mixture. Let the shrimp sit while you move forward with the spicy black bean soup.

Add the black beans to the skillet with the onions. With a potato masher or the back of a rubber spatula, smash the equivalent of half of the beans—the mashed-up beans will thicken the soup. Add the fire-roasted tomatoes, chicken stock, and heavy cream (if using) to the pot, stir, and turn the heat up a bit to bring the soup up to a bubble. Once at a bubble, turn the heat back down to a simmer and let it cook for 10 to 12 minutes. Give the pot a stir every now and then to ensure that it is not sticking.

While the soup is simmering, preheat a large skillet over medium-high heat. Once it is hot add the shrimp and cook them for 2 to 3 minutes on the first side. Flip the shrimp, add the lime juice, and continue to cook them for 2 to 3 more minutes or until the shrimp are opaque.

Taste the soup and adjust the seasoning with salt, pepper, and hot sauce. To serve it, place a few ladles full of the spicy black bean soup in shallow soup bowls, and arrange 4 shrimp standing up in the center of each bowl.

And make sure you have the following On Hand:

EVOO • Onion • Garlic • Chili powder • Ground cumin • Salt and black pepper • Red pepper flakes • Limes • Flat-leaf parsley • Canned black beans • Canned diced fire-roasted tomatoes • Chicken stock • Heavy cream (optional) • Hot sauce

Sweet Soy-Soaked Salmon Fillets Over Noodle-y Veggies

Guilt-free pasta? Everything is a pasta-bility when you add fresh fish and lots of veggies.

4 SERVINGS

Salt

½ pound of the thinnest long-cut pasta you have on hand

6 tablespoons tamari

3-inch piece fresh ginger, peeled and grated

Juice of 1 lime, plus more to taste

¼ teaspoon red pepper flakes (eyeball it)

4 salmon fillets

1 large bundle broccolini

1 large carrot

4 to 5 garlic cloves

1 large red bell pepper

4 scallions, trimmed

4 tablespoons vegetable oil

2 teaspoons sugar

¾ cup chicken stock

Place a large pot of water with a tight-fitting lid over high heat and bring to a boil. Once it comes up to a boil, add salt and pasta. Cook the pasta according to package directions to al dente. Drain thoroughly.

While the pasta works, in a shallow dish combine the tamari, ginger, lime juice, and the red pepper flakes. Add the salmon fillets, turn to coat, and marinate for about 5 minutes.

Trim the broccolini ends. Place 2 to 3 inches of water in a large nonstick skillet; add salt to the water along with the trimmed broccolini. Cover with a lid or some aluminum foil and bring up to a bubble; simmer for 4 to 5 minutes, until tender.

While the broccolini is cooking, chop up the rest of the veggies and reserve them on your cutting board or on a plate: peel and grate the carrot, finely chop the garlic, seed and thinly slice the red bell pepper. Thinly slice both the white and green parts of the scallions down to the roots and reserve separately.

Drain the broccolini and reserve. Return the skillet to the stove over medium-high heat and add 2 tablespoons of the vegetable oil, twice around the pan. Remove the salmon fillets from the marinade, reserving the marinade, and add the salmon to the hot skillet, skin side down. Cook the salmon until it has just cooked through, about 3 to 4 minutes on each side.

Remove the salmon to a plate and cover it with a piece of aluminum foil to keep it warm. Wipe the skillet out and return it to the stove over medium-high heat; add the remaining 2 tablespoons of oil. Add the garlic, bell pepper, and grated carrots, and cook for about 2 minutes, stirring frequently. Add the sugar to the reserved salmon marinade, stir it to combine, then add it to the skillet. Add the cooked broccolini and the chicken stock, bring the liquids up to a bubble, and let them simmer for 1 minute. Add the cooked, drained pasta and the scallions and toss to combine. Taste for seasoning and add more tamari and lime juice to taste if the flavor is not strong enough for you.

To serve, divide the noodles and veggies among 4 serving plates and top with the salmon.

EXPRESS LANE
SHOPPING LIST

❑ **3-inch piece** fresh ginger

❑ **4 salmon fillets,**
   6 ounces each

❑ **1 large bundle** broccolini
   (1 to 1¼ pounds)

❑ **1 large red** bell pepper

❑ **1 bunch** scallions

And make sure you have
the following On Hand:

Salt • Long-cut pasta •
Tamari • Lime • Red pepper
flakes • Carrot • Garlic
• Vegetable oil • Sugar •
Chicken stock

Lamb Chops and Spaghetti Salad with Raw Cherry Tomato Sauce

I recently ate at a wonderful little bistro in Montreal called Chez L'Epicier, or "house of the grocer." The menus are written on what look like grocery sacks. Well, supper here was so good, I went out and got a sack of my own groceries to make a 30-Minute Meal knock-off of their gourmet lamb shank served with "raw spaghetti," which turned out to be pasta with raw sauce. Hey, Montreal is a favorite getaway of mine, but I can make this meal any night I like and my market's a lot closer!

4 SERVINGS

EVOO (extra-virgin olive oil) for drizzling plus about $^{1}/_{3}$ cup, eyeball it

2 pounds **loin lamb chops**, 1 to 1$^{1}/_{2}$ inches thick

Salt and **black pepper**

1 pound **spaghetti** or other long-cut pasta

3 tablespoons **balsamic vinegar**, eyeball it

1 large **garlic clove**, finely chopped

4 **scallions**, finely chopped

3 tablespoons fresh **mint leaves** (a handful), minced

1 pint **grape** or **small cherry tomatoes**, halved

1 cup grated **Pecorino Romano cheese** (a few generous handfuls)

Bring a large pot of water to boil for the pasta.

Preheat the broiler and set the broiler pan 6 inches from the flame. Drizzle a bit of EVOO over the chops and season them liberally on both sides with salt and pepper.

When the water comes to a boil, salt it then add the spaghetti and cook to al dente. While the pasta cooks, combine the vinegar, ⅓ cup of EVOO, garlic, scallions, and mint in a large bowl with the tomatoes.

Place the chops under the broiler and cook a few minutes on each side for rare, 6 minutes on each side for medium to medium well; the time will vary depending on your broiler and the thickness of the chops. (Rare feels like the fleshy part of your hand near your thumb. Medium to medium-well will have some give but the meat will be firm.) Let the meat rest for 3 or 4 minutes before serving to allow the juices to redistribute.

Drain the pasta well and toss with the tomatoes and dressing. Sprinkle with the cheese and grind lots of black pepper over the pasta, then toss again and add salt to taste. Serve a pile of the spaghetti salad alongside a couple of chops per serving.

Brutus Salad

This is my latest version of what has become one of my classic 30-Minute-Meals, Beefy Brutus Salad, a Caesar-style salad with Italian thin-cut steak! Why should chicken have all the fun?

4 SERVINGS

1½ pounds very thin cut, ½-inch thick, **shell steak** (2 large, thin steaks)

EVOO (extra-virgin olive oil) for drizzling plus ⅓ cup (eyeball it)

1 tablespoons finely chopped **rosemary**, a few sprigs

1 tablespoon (a palmful) **grill seasoning** such as McCormick's Montreal Steak Seasoning

A large crusty **semolina roll** or ½ small semolina loaf

2 **garlic cloves**, cracked away from skin

Black pepper

Juice of 1 lemon

2 teaspoons **Dijon mustard**

2 teaspoons **Worcestershire sauce** (eyeball it)

1 teaspoon **hot sauce**, such as Tabasco (eyeball it)

2 teaspoons **anchovy paste** (a must for me, optional for you)

3 **hearts of romaine**, chopped

1 cup grated **Parmigiano-Reggiano** or Pecorino Romano cheese (a few generous handfuls)

Preheat the broiler.

Set the meat out on the counter to get the chill off it from the fridge while you heat a grill pan over high heat. Drizzle the steak with EVOO and rub it with the rosemary and grill seasoning. Grill for 3 minutes on each side—these steaks are really thin—then transfer the meat to a plate and let it rest to allow the juices to redistribute.

Toast the split roll or bread under the broiler until deeply golden, then rub with one clove of cracked, split garlic. Drizzle EVOO over the bread and season with a little pepper, then chop the bread into cubes.

Rub the inside of a bowl with the remaining cracked clove of garlic, then mince up the garlic and add it to the bowl. Whisk in the lemon juice, mustard, Worcestershire, hot sauce, and anchovy paste, then whisk in 1/3 cup of EVOO. Add the greens and bread to the bowl and toss to coat with the dressing. Add the cheese to the salad and toss again, then season with black pepper to taste. Top servings of the salad with slices of steak or serve the meat alongside.

Italian Cobb Salad

I really love grilled chicken salad as a go-to, no-brainer supper solution, but the Chicken Caesar is so over for me—I need a few years off! So here's another fresh chicken salad idea; eat your heart out, Caesar!

4 SERVINGS

3 tablespoons **balsamic vinegar**

6 tablespoons **EVOO** (extra-virgin olive oil)

1 tablespoon finely chopped **thyme** leaves, a few sprigs

4 boneless, skinless **chicken breasts**

1 tablespoon **grill seasoning**, such as McCormick's Montreal Steak Seasoning

1 rounded teaspoonful **Dijon mustard**

A few drops **hot sauce**, such as Tabasco

2 **hearts of romaine**, chopped

Salt and **black pepper**

1 can quartered **artichoke hearts** in water, drained

4 **hard-boiled eggs**

½ pound deli-sliced **Genoa salami** or soppressata, cut into strips

¾ pound **gorgonzola cheese**, crumbled

Hot peppers, such as pepperoncini or hot Italian cherry peppers, chopped

Preheat a grill pan or large nonstick skillet over medium high heat.

Combine 1 tablespoon of the balsamic vinegar and 3 tablespoons of the EVOO on a plate and add the thyme. Coat the chicken evenly in the dressing, then season the meat liberally on both sides with the grill seasoning. Add the chicken to the hot pan and cook for 6 minutes on each side.

While the chicken cooks, add the remaining 2 tablespoons of balsamic vinegar to the bottom of a large, shallow serving bowl. Whisk in the mustard, hot sauce, and remaining 3 tablespoons of EVOO. Transfer the cooked chicken to a cutting board, let it rest for a couple of minutes, then slice it on an angle. Set aside to cool slightly.

Add the greens to the serving bowl and toss with the dressing; season with salt and pepper to taste. Arrange the artichokes, hard-boiled eggs, salami, and gorgonzola on top of the salad in rows, with a row of cooled chicken slices down the middle. Scatter a few chopped hot peppers over the salad and serve.

Spicy Sausage Meatloaf Patties with Italian Barbecue Sauce

When I made my annual Christmas Pasta for the holiday this year we discovered that both my mom and I had shopped for the ingredients, so we had lots of leftover hot and sweet sausage and ground beef in the fridge. The next day, this recipe was born.

MAKES 4 BIG PATTIES

- 2 tablespoons **EVOO** (extra virgin olive oil) plus some for drizzling
- 1 **red bell pepper**, cored, seeded, and finely chopped
- 1 large **onion**, chopped
- 2 **celery ribs**, chopped
- 1 small **carrot**, peeled and chopped
- **Salt** and **black pepper**
- ¾ pound **bulk hot sausage**
- ¾ pound **bulk sweet sausage**
- ½ pound **ground beef**
- 1 **egg**
- ¾ cup **bread crumbs** (3 generous handfuls), Italian or plain
- ½ cup grated **Parmigiano-Reggiano** or Pecorino Romano cheese (a couple of handfuls)
- ⅛ pound **pancetta** (4 slices), chopped
- 3 **garlic cloves**, chopped
- ½ cup **beef stock**
- 1 can **petite-diced tomatoes** or stewed tomatoes
- 1 tablespoon **Worcestershire sauce**
- 2 teaspoons **hot sauce**
- 6 cups **mixed greens**

Preheat the oven to 425°F.

Heat a small skillet over medium heat with 2 tablespoons of the EVOO. When the oil is hot, add the red bell pepper, half the onion, celery, and carrots and sauté together for 5 minutes. Season with salt and pepper, then remove to a plate to cool.

Combine the sausage and ground beef with the egg, bread crumbs, cheese, and cooled sautéed vegetables, mixing well. Form 4 large oval-shaped patties no more than 1¼ inches thick and arrange them on a cookie sheet. Drizzle the patties with EVOO and bake for 17 to 18 minutes, until cooked through.

Heat a medium saucepot over medium high heat. Add a drizzle of EVOO to the pan, and add then the pancetta. Let the pancetta crisp up a bit and render its fat, then add the remaining chopped onion and the garlic and cook until tender, 8 to 10 minutes. Stir in the beef stock and tomatoes and season the sauce heavily with coarsely ground black pepper. Add the Worcestershire and hot sauce and reduce the heat to low.

Serve the meatloaf patties topped with the Italian barbecue sauce and a green salad alongside.

```
1.25 lb @ 0.79 /lb
IT              CARROTS 4562
2 @ 2.69
                SEV GNOCCHI
2 @ 1.79
                DOUGH BALLS
                CORN MUFFINS
5 @ 2.49
                SWANSONS
2 @ 2.49
                SWANSN BROTH
2 @ 2.50
```

BRING IT ON! (BUT, BE GENTLE.)

Even after taping four shows in one day there are nights I cannot wait to get home to my family and my stove—I really do *love* to cook. Cooking centers me and oftentimes the busier I am the more the act of preparing a meal helps me focus and figure out that day's piece of my big picture. The meals in this section are elaborate only in presentation. You may be called upon to watch more than one pot, but in less than 30 minutes and with fewer than 10 ingredients (in addition to some ingredients from your On Hand list) you will revel in one mean meal. Try my favorites, the Drunken Tuscan Pasta or my wedding meal, the Montalcino Chicken with Figs and Buttered Gnocchi with Nutmeg. Your friends will say bring it on!

Good Fennels Pasta

I make this one when I watch *GoodFellas.* Shave the garlic nice and thin, like Paulie would, but don't use a razor blade like he does in the movie. A sharp knife is fine.

4 SERVINGS

　　Salt

1　pound **bucatini** (hollow fat spaghetti) or other long-cut pasta

3　tablespoons **EVOO** (extra-virgin olive oil)

1　pound **bulk sweet Italian sausage**

4　**garlic cloves**, very thinly sliced

1　medium **onion**, very thinly sliced

1　**fennel bulb**, trimmed, quartered, cored, and very thinly sliced

2　**cubanelle peppers**, seeded and very thinly sliced

　　Black pepper

1　cup **dry white wine** or stock (eyeball it)

1　28-ounce can **crushed tomatoes**, such as San Marzano

½　cup grated **Parmigiano-Reggiano** cheese (eyeball it), plus some to pass at the table

1　cup fresh **basil**, 20 leaves, shredded or torn

　　Crusty bread, for mopping

❑ 1 pound bulk sweet Italian
sausage

❑ 1 fennel bulb

❑ 2 cubanelle peppers

❑ 1 bunch fresh basil

❑ 1 loaf crusty bread

Place a large pot of water on to boil for the pasta. Salt the water and add the bucatini and cook it to al dente.

While the water comes to a boil and the pasta cooks, make the sauce. Heat a large, deep nonstick skillet over medium-high heat. Add 1 tablespoon of the EVOO, once around the pan. Add the sausage to the skillet and break up the sausage into small bits. Brown the sausage all over, then transfer it to a paper-towel-lined plate. Return the pan to the heat and add the remaining 2 tablespoons of EVOO, the garlic, onions, fennel, and peppers. Season the vegetables with salt and pepper. Cook, turning frequently, 7 to 8 minutes, until tender, but do not allow the fennel and onions to brown. Reduce the heat a bit if they begin to. Add the wine or stock next and reduce for 2 minutes. Stir in the tomatoes and slide the sausage back into the pan. Reduce the heat to a simmer and cook until the pasta is done.

Drain the pasta very well and add it to the sauce. Sprinkle the pasta with $1/2$ cup cheese (a couple of handfuls), then toss the pasta with the thick sauce to combine. Transfer the pasta to a large shallow platter and cover the pasta with basil leaves. Serve it with extra cheese and pass crusty bread at the table to mop up the plates.

And make sure you have the following On Hand:

Salt • Long-cut pasta, preferably bucatini • EVOO • Garlic • Onion • Black pepper • White wine • Canned crushed tomatoes • Parmigiano-Reggiano cheese

Drunken Tuscan Pasta

Pasta stewed up in red wine is a Tuscan invention: my kinda people! I toss it together with other usual suspects from the region: wild mushrooms, rosemary, and dark greens.

4 SERVINGS

1 bottle **Tuscan red table wine** such as Rosso di Montalcino or Chianti

Coarse salt

1 pound **perciatelli**, bucatini, or spaghetti (dried long-cut pasta)

3 tablespoons **EVOO** (extra-virgin olive oil)

¼ pound deli-sliced **pancetta** (see Note)

3 **portobello mushroom caps**, thinly sliced

2 to 3 sprigs fresh **rosemary**, leaves finely chopped

4 **garlic cloves**, chopped

A couple pinches of **red pepper flakes**

4 to 5 cups **chopped dark greens**, your choice of chard, escarole, spinach, or kale

Black pepper, to taste

¼ teaspoon freshly grated **nutmeg**

Grated **Parmigiano-Reggiano** cheese, a handful plus some to pass at the table

NOTE: Three bacon slices may be substituted for the pancetta. They are similar in that both are cured pork, the difference being that bacon is also smoked.

Pour the entire bottle of wine into a large pot. Add water and fill the pot up as you would to cook pasta. Bring the wine and water to a boil over high heat. When the liquids boil, add salt and the pasta and cook to al dente. Heads up: you will ladle out some cooking liquid for the pasta sauce before draining the pasta.

Heat a large nonstick skillet over medium heat. Add 2 tablespoons of the EVOO, twice around the pan, then chop and add the pancetta. Brown the pieces until they are golden at the edges and transfer them to a paper-towel-lined plate. Add the mushrooms to the EVOO in the same skillet, season them with the chopped rosemary, and cook until they are deeply golden, 6 to 8 minutes. Push the mushrooms to the sides of the pan and add the remaining tablespoon of EVOO to the center of the skillet. Add the garlic and red pepper flakes to the EVOO and cook them for a minute or so, then toss the mushrooms together with the garlic. Add the greens to the pan and season them with salt, pepper, and the nutmeg. When the greens have wilted down, add a couple of ladles of the starchy pasta cooking liquid to the pan and cook for a minute to reduce it a little.

Drain the pasta well and add it to the skillet. Add the pancetta and a handful of cheese to the pan. Toss the pasta for a minute or so to allow it to absorb the remaining liquid. Adjust the seasonings and serve. Pass the extra cheese at the table.

EXPRESS LANE SHOPPING LIST

- ¼ pound deli-sliced pancetta (see Note)
- 3 portobello mushroom caps
- Fresh rosemary, 2 to 3 sprigs
- 1 large bunch or 2 small bunches dark, leafy greens, your choice of chard, escarole, spinach, or kale

FROM THE LIQUOR STORE

- Tuscan red table wine or other dry red wine from your on hand

---

And make sure you have the following On Hand:

Coarse salt • Long-cut pasta, such as perciatelli, bucatini, or spaghetti • EVOO • Garlic • Red pepper flakes • Black pepper • Nutmeg • Parmigiano-Reggiano cheese

Sweet Soy-Glazed Chicken with Carrot-Sesame Noodles (MYOTO)

Here's another MYOTO (make your own take-out). Thai this one, you'll surely like it.

4 SERVINGS

Salt

1 pound **thin long-cut pasta**, such as vermicelli

¼ cup **tamari** plus 1 tablespoon (eyeball it)

4 tablespoons **brown sugar**

1¾ cups **chicken stock**

Juice of 1 lime

4 large **garlic cloves**, 1 crushed, 3 chopped

3-inch piece of **fresh ginger**, peeled and grated or finely chopped

½ teaspoon **red pepper flakes** (eyeball it)

2 tablespoons **vegetable oil**, plus some for drizzling

1 large yellow **onion**, chopped

1 pound **carrots**, peeled and shredded with a box grater or the grating blade on a food processor

Freshly ground black pepper

6 thin-cut **chicken breast cutlets**

1 teaspoon **toasted sesame oil**

¼ cup **toasted sesame seeds**

¼ cup fresh **cilantro leaves**, a generous handful, chopped

½ cup fresh **basil**, 10 leaves, chopped or torn

¼ cup fresh **flat-leaf parsley**, a generous handful, chopped

Preheat a grill pan or outdoor grill over high heat.

Place a large pot of water with a tight-fitting lid over high heat and bring it to a boil. Once it comes up to a boil, add some salt and the pasta. Cook the pasta until al dente. Drain and reserve it.

While the water is coming up to a boil, make the soy glaze. In a small skillet, combine the ¼ cup of tamari, the brown sugar, ¼ cup of the chicken stock, the lime juice, crushed garlic clove, one fourth of the grated ginger, and the red pepper flakes. Place it over medium-high heat, bring it up to a simmer, and cook it until the glaze looks like a watery syrup, about 3 to 4 minutes, then remove it from the heat and reserve.

Preheat a large skillet over medium-high heat with 2 tablespoons of the vegetable oil, twice around the pan. Add the onions, carrots, chopped garlic, the remaining ginger, a little salt, and a generous amount of pepper; cook for 5 minutes, stirring frequently. If the pan starts to look dry, add a bit more oil.

While the carrots are cooking, grill the chicken. Season the chicken with some pepper and drizzle it with a little oil. Place the seasoned chicken cutlets on the grill and cook for 3 to 4 minutes or until well marked, then flip the chicken and brush with the soy glaze. Continue to cook it for another 3 to 4 minutes, or until it is cooked through. Brush again with the glaze, flip it, and then brush one last time with the glaze. Remove the grilled chicken to a plate, tent it with a piece of foil, and let it rest a few minutes while you pull together the carrots and noodles.

Add the remaining 1½ cups of chicken stock and the remaining tablespoon of tamari to the carrots, bring them up to a bubble, and simmer for 1 minute. Add the drained pasta, stir to combine them, and cook for about 30 seconds so the pasta soaks in some of the sauce. Turn the heat off and drizzle the mixture with the toasted sesame oil, then sprinkle it with the toasted sesame seeds, cilantro, basil, and parsley. Toss thoroughly to combine. Taste and adjust the seasonings with a little more sesame oil, salt, and pepper and transfer it to a platter. Slice the chicken into thin strips and arrange them on top of the carrot-sesame noodles.

EXPRESS LANE
SHOPPING LIST

❏ 3-inch piece of fresh ginger
❏ 6 thin-cut chicken breast cutlets
❏ 1 bottle toasted sesame oil
❏ 1 small jar toasted sesame seeds
❏ 1 bunch fresh cilantro
❏ 1 bunch fresh basil

And make sure you have the following On Hand:

Salt • Thin long-cut pasta, such as vermicelli • Tamari • Brown sugar • Chicken stock • Lime • Garlic • Red pepper flakes • Vegetable oil • Onion • Carrots • Freshly ground black pepper • Flat-leaf parsley

Spanish Pork Chops with Linguica Corn Stuffing and Cherry–Red Wine Gravy

Confession: I have never been to Spain. This is actually my version of a fantabulous meal I enjoyed at a late-night hot spot in Vancouver, north of the border. It's good because you get salty, sweet, and savory in each and every bite. Note to self: gotta go to Spain. I serve these with green beans.

4 SERVINGS

- 4 thick **boneless center-cut pork chops**, about 2 pounds
  Salt and **black pepper**
- 3 tablespoons **EVOO** (extra-virgin olive oil)
- 2 tablespoons **butter**
- 2 tablespoons **all-purpose flour**
- 1 cup **dry red wine** (eyeball it; about ¼ bottle)
- ½ cup **black cherry preserves** or all-fruit spread
- 2 cups **beef stock**
- ½ pound **linguica** or chorizo, chopped
- 2 **celery ribs**, chopped
- 1 medium **onion**, chopped
- 2 **garlic cloves**, chopped
- 1 small red **bell pepper**, cored, seeded, and chopped
- 4 **corn muffins**, crumbled
- 1 teaspoon **smoked paprika**, ⅓ palmful
- 2 tablespoons chopped fresh **thyme leaves**, from 4 to 5 sprigs
- 1 pound **green beans**, stem ends trimmed
  A handful of fresh **flat-leaf parsley**, chopped

> **TIDBIT**
> Rioja is a grape specific to Spain. Riojas come in both white and red and they are affordable. However, any dry red wine can be used. But since flavors get concentrated when wine is cooked, make sure the wine is one that you'd like to drink in a glass.

Preheat the oven to 350°F.

Heat a skillet over medium-high heat. Season the pork chops with salt and pepper. Add 2 tablespoons of the EVOO, twice around the pan. Add the chops and caramelize the meat for 2 minutes on each side. Transfer the chops to a baking sheet and put in the oven to finish cooking through, 12 to 15 minutes. Add the butter to the same skillet and reduce the heat a bit. Add the flour and cook for 1 minute. Whisk the wine into the pan and cook for 1 minute, then whisk in the preserves and 1 cup of the stock. Season with salt and pepper and let the gravy thicken over low heat.

Heat a medium nonstick skillet over medium-high heat with the remaining tablespoon of EVOO. When the oil smokes, add the linguica or chorizo and brown it for 2 minutes. Add the celery, onions, garlic, and bell peppers, and season them with salt and pepper. Cook for 5 minutes, then crumble the muffins into the skillet and combine with the vegetables. Dampen the stuffing with the remaining cup of stock and season with the paprika and thyme. Reduce the heat to low and keep the stuffing warm until it is ready to serve.

Heat 1 inch of water in a skillet and add salt and the beans. Cook for 4 to 5 minutes, until the beans are tender, then drain.

Remove the meat from the oven and whisk the drippings into your gravy. Pile the stuffing on plates with the chops alongside and ladle the gravy over both. Scatter the parsley over the meat and stuffing. Serve with the green beans.

Not-sagna Pasta Toss

Easier than lasagna, because it's *not* lasagna, this pasta, meat sauce, and ricotta toss-up is just as hearty and comforting as the layered Italian fave, but it's ready in a fraction of the time and with much less effort. Serve with a simple green salad dressed with oil and vinegar.

4 SERVINGS

Coarse salt

1 pound curly **short-cut pasta**, such as campanelle by Barilla, or cavatappi (hollow corkscrew pasta)

2 tablespoons **EVOO** (extra-virgin olive oil), twice around the pan

1 pound **ground sirloin**

1 medium **onion**, finely chopped

4 **garlic cloves**, chopped

½ teaspoon **red pepper flakes** (eyeball it in your palm)

Black pepper

½ teaspoon **ground allspice** (eyeball it in your palm)

1 teaspoon **Worcestershire sauce**

½ cup **dry red wine**, a couple of glugs

½ cup **beef stock**

1 28-ounce can **crushed tomatoes**

1½ cups **part-skim ricotta cheese**

½ cup grated **Parmigiano-Reggiano** cheese, a couple of handfuls, plus some to pass at the table

1 cup fresh **basil**, about 20 leaves

Bring a large pot of water to a boil for the pasta. Salt the water and cook the pasta to al dente. Heads up: you will need a ladle of the starchy cooking water to help form the sauce before you drain the pasta.

Heat a deep nonstick skillet over medium-high heat. Add the EVOO, then the meat. Break it up into small bits and cook for 4 to 5 minutes, or until the meat has good color to it. Add the onions, garlic, and red pepper flakes and season them with salt, pepper, the allspice, and the Worcestershire sauce. Cook for another 5 minutes, deglaze the meat and onions with the red wine, cook off a minute, then stir the stock into the meat. Stir in the tomatoes and bring it to a bubble. Reduce the heat to medium low and simmer for 5 minutes.

Place the ricotta cheese in the bottom of a shallow bowl. Add a ladleful of boiling, starchy pasta water to the ricotta and stir to combine them. Add a couple of handfuls of grated Parm cheese to the ricotta and mix it in.

Drain the pasta. Toss the hot pasta with the cheeses. Add half of the thick meat sauce to the pasta bowl and toss again to combine. Tear or shred the basil and add it to the meat and pasta, then toss them again. Taste it to adjust the salt and pepper. Serve bowlfuls of Not-sagna with extra sauce on top and more grated Parm to pass at the table.

EXPRESS LANE
SHOPPING LIST

❑ **1 pound ground sirloin**

❑ **1 15-ounce container part-skim ricotta cheese**

❑ **1 bunch fresh basil**

And make sure you have the following On Hand:

Coarse salt • Short-cut pasta • EVOO • Onion • Garlic • Red pepper flakes • Black pepper • Ground allspice • Worcestershire • Dry red wine • Beef stock • Canned crushed tomatoes • Parmigiano-Reggiano cheese

Vegetable Not-sagna Pasta Toss

Like the title says, this is lasagna but it's not. Veggie lasagna is often served up layered with a creamy white sauce and seasonal vegetables. This dish incorporates vegetables, ricotta, and a just-creamy-enough sauce tossed with pasta—without all the work and the long baking time.

4 SERVINGS

Coarse salt

1 pound curly **short-cut pasta**, such as campanelle by Barilla, or cavatappi (hollow corkscrew pasta)

1 10-ounce box **frozen chopped spinach**

3 tablespoons **EVOO** (extra-virgin olive oil)

1 medium **zucchini**

12 **cremini** or baby portobello mushrooms, sliced

1 medium **onion**, thinly sliced

3 **garlic cloves**, chopped

Black pepper

1 **jarred roasted red pepper**, drained, patted dry, quartered lengthwise, then thinly sliced

1 tablespoon **butter**

2 rounded tablespoons **all-purpose flour**

1 cup **chicken stock**

1 cup **milk**

¼ teaspoon freshly **grated nutmeg** (eyeball it)

1½ cups **part-skim ricotta cheese**

½ cup grated **Parmigiano-Reggiano** cheese, a couple of handfuls, plus some to pass at the table

1 cup fresh **basil**, about 20 leaves

Bring a pot of water to a boil for the pasta. Salt the boiling water and cook the pasta to al dente. Heads up: you will need a ladle of the hot cooking water just before you drain the pasta.

Place the frozen spinach on a plate and microwave on high for 6 minutes to defrost it. Place the defrosted spinach in a clean kitchen towel and wring the liquid out of it.

Heat a deep skillet over medium-high heat and add 2 tablespoons of the EVOO, twice around the pan. Halve the zucchini lengthwise, then thinly slice it into half moons and add it to the pan with the mushrooms. Cook for 2 to 3 minutes, then add the onions and garlic. Season the vegetables with salt and pepper. When the onions are tender, about 5 minutes, add the defrosted spinach, separating it into small bits, and the roasted red peppers. Toss to heat them through. Transfer the veggies to a dish and return the skillet to the stovetop. Add the remaining tablespoon of EVOO and the butter. When the butter melts into the EVOO, add the flour to the fat and cook for a minute or so, then whisk in the stock and the milk. Bring the sauce to a bubble and cook for 2 to 3 minutes, until reduced and thickened. Season the sauce with salt, pepper, and nutmeg. Slide the vegetables back into the sauce.

Place the part-skim ricotta in a large shallow bowl and combine it with a ladle of boiling, starchy pasta cooking water. Add a couple of handfuls of the grated Parm cheese.

Drain the pasta and toss it with the cheeses. Add half the vegetables and sauce to the pasta and toss them to combine. Tear or shred the basil and toss it into the pasta. Adjust the seasonings. Top the bowlfuls of Vegetable Not-sagna with the remaining veggies in the sauce and pass the extra grated cheese at the table.

EXPRESS LANE
SHOPPING LIST

❑ 1 medium zucchini

❑ 12 cremini or baby portobello mushrooms

❑ 1 15-ounce container part-skim ricotta cheese

❑ 1 bunch fresh basil

And make sure you have the following On Hand:

Coarse salt • Short-cut pasta • Frozen chopped spinach • EVOO • Onion • Garlic • Black pepper • Jarred roasted red pepper • Butter • Flour • Chicken stock • Milk • Nutmeg • Parmigiano-Reggiano cheese

Crisp Red Snapper and Sweet Winter Stir-Fry Vegetables

I often throw holiday parties with a casual theme. This dish was the centerpiece of a holiday-style Make Your Own Take-out gathering. You will never find anything like this delivered to your door in a brown paper sack, but if you do a little bit of chopping you'll be famous for many holidays to come. P.S. Don't wait for a holiday to make it.

4 SERVINGS

3 **beets**, medium to large, yellow, orange, or red

   Salt

4 **red snapper fillets**, 6 to 8 ounces each, patted dry

   Black pepper

2 teaspoons **ground coriander**

½ cup **cornstarch**, for dusting (eyeball the amount on a plate)

   Vegetable oil, for shallow frying, plus 2 tablespoons, twice around the pan

2 medium **zucchini**, cut into sticks about 3 inches long and ½ inch wide

6 **scallions**, cut into 3-inch pieces, then thinly sliced lengthwise

   2-inch piece **fresh ginger**, peeled and grated or minced

4 **garlic cloves**, chopped

2 pinches **red pepper flakes**

1 cup **duck sauce**, from the Asian foods aisle

2 **limes**, one juiced, one cut into wedges

❑ 3 medium to large beets,
   yellow, orange, or red

❑ 4 red snapper fillets,
   6 to 8 ounces each

❑ 1 box cornstarch

❑ 2 medium zucchini

❑ 1 bunch scallions

❑ 2-inch piece fresh ginger

❑ 1 jar duck sauce, from the
   Asian foods aisle

Cut off the ends of the beets and stand them upright on a cutting board. Peel each beet in strips, cutting it from top to bottom and turning the beet as you trim. Then slice the beets ½ inch thick and place the slices in a pot. Cover them with water, bring the water to a boil, and add salt. Cook the beets for 5 minutes, drain them, run them under cold water and pat them dry. Slice them into ½-inch-thick sticks.

While the beets cook, score the skin of the fish fillets by making a few shallow parallel cuts. The skin will get crispy and delicious, and scoring it will keep it from curling. Season the snapper by sprinkling some salt and pepper and the coriander evenly over the flesh side of the fillets. Pour out the cornstarch in a shallow dish. Dust the fish on both sides with cornstarch. Discard the excess.

Cover the bottom of one large nonstick skillet with a ⅛-inch layer of oil. Turn the heat on high. Add 2 tablespoons of oil to a second skillet and heat it to high as well.

When the oil ripples in the first skillet, add the fish fillets and cook them for 3 to 4 minutes on each side, until they are crisp and firm.

To the second hot skillet, while the snapper cooks, add the zucchini and stir-fry for 3 to 4 minutes, then add the beets, scallions, ginger, garlic, and red pepper flakes and cook them for a minute or two more. Add the duck sauce to the pan and heat through, glazing the veggies. Add the lime juice to the skillet and remove the skillet from the heat. Serve the fish over the veggies and pass the lime wedges at the table.

And make sure you have the following On Hand:

Salt • Black pepper • Ground coriander • Cornstarch • Vegetable oil • Garlic • Red pepper flakes • Limes

Deluxe, Divine Chicken Divan

This dish is what I call a "Retro Metro." Back in the day, Chicken Divan—poultry, poulet sauce, broccoli, and mushrooms—was a continental cuisine staple. As a special treat, my mom would take me to NYC to the Magic Pan for Chicken Divan Crepes. This is an easy cosmopolitan update on the classic. The broccoli is swapped out for asparagus and the preparation time is reduced. Enjoy!

4 SERVINGS

- ⅓ cup **sliced almonds**, a couple of handfuls
- 1 quart **chicken stock**
- **Zest of 1 lemon**
- 3 to 4 fresh **thyme sprigs**
- 4 tablespoons (½ stick) **butter**
- 1½ cups **white rice**
- 8 **chicken breast cutlets**
- **Salt** and **black pepper**
- 1 teaspoon **poultry seasoning**, ⅓ palmful
- 2 rounded tablespoons plus about ½ cup **all-purpose flour**
- 2 tablespoons **EVOO** (extra-virgin olive oil), twice around the pan
- 1 large bunch **asparagus**, trimmed of tough ends
- 6 to 8 large **white mushrooms**, sliced
- ⅓ cup **white wine** (eyeball it)
- ⅓ cup **half-and-half** or heavy cream
- 1 rounded tablespoon **Dijon mustard**
- 2 tablespoons fresh **tarragon**, a couple of sprigs, chopped
- 2 **scallions**, chopped

Toast the almonds in a small skillet until they are golden, then reserve them.

Bring 2¾ cups of the chicken stock, the lemon zest, thyme sprigs, and a tablespoon of the butter to a boil in a medium pot with a tight-fitting lid. Add the rice to the water and stir. Return the water to a boil, then reduce the heat to a simmer and cover the pot. Cook it for 18 minutes, or until tender, then remove it from the heat. Remove the thyme sprigs; the leaves will have fallen off in the rice.

While the rice cooks, season the chicken with salt, pepper, and the poultry seasoning. Dredge the chicken in about ½ cup flour, then discard the excess. Heat a large skillet over medium to medium-high heat. Add the EVOO and 1 tablespoon of the butter to the large skillet. To the hot butter and oil, add the cutlets and cook for 3 to 4 minutes on each side. Remove the meat to a large platter and cover it with foil to keep it warm.

Bring an inch or two of water to a simmer in a shallow pan and season it with salt. Add the asparagus and cook it for 4 minutes, or until it is just tender but still bright green. Remove it and add it to the chicken platter to keep it warm.

Return the chicken skillet to the heat and add the remaining 2 tablespoons of butter. Melt the butter, add the mushrooms and cook until soft, about 5 minutes. Whisk in 2 rounded tablespoons of flour. Cook the flour for 1 minute, then whisk in the wine. Cook off the wine, 30 seconds, then whisk in the remaining 1¼ cups of chicken stock and the half-and-half. When the sauce bubbles, stir in the mustard and tarragon and let the sauce simmer and thicken for 2 to 3 minutes.

Stir the scallions into the rice and fluff with a fork. Make a bed of rice on each dinner plate. Top it with a serving of steamed asparagus, then 2 chicken cutlets. Cover the chicken with the tarragon sauce, allowing the gravy to spill over the edges into the asparagus and rice. Sprinkle the plates with toasted nuts. Wow! Can you believe you made this?

Black Cherry–Black Pepper Lamb Chops with Sweet Pea Risotto

This is a great date meal for your Lamb Chop, Sweet Pea, or Honey Pie. No need to worry about dessert—you're it!

4 SERVINGS

- 1 quart **chicken stock**
- 2 tablespoons **butter**
- 2 tablespoons **EVOO** (extra-virgin olive oil), plus some for drizzling
- 1 small **onion**, chopped
- 2 **garlic cloves**, chopped
- 1 cup **Arborio rice**
- ½ cup **white wine**
- 1 cup **frozen green peas**, a couple of overflowing handfuls
- ½ cup grated **Parmigiano-Reggiano** cheese, a couple of handfuls
- 2 tablespoons chopped fresh **mint**, plus a few sprigs for garnish

  A handful of fresh **flat-leaf parsley**, chopped
- 4 **loin lamb chops**, each 1½ inches thick
- 1 **shallot**, thinly sliced
- ½ cup **black cherry all-fruit preserves**
- 3 tablespoons **balsamic vinegar**
- ½ teaspoon **cracked black pepper** (eyeball it in your palm)

  Salt

❑ 1 box Arborio rice

❑ 1 bunch fresh mint

❑ 4 loin lamb chops,
    1½ inches thick

❑ 1 jar black cherry all-fruit
    preserves, such as
    Polaner brand

Place the stock in a medium pot and warm it up over medium-low heat.

Place an oven rack 8 inches from the broiler and preheat the broiler to high.

In a medium skillet over medium to medium-high heat, melt a tablespoon of the butter with a tablespoon of the EVOO, once around the pan. When the pan is hot, add the onions and garlic and cook for 2 to 3 minutes, then add the Arborio and cook for a minute more. Add the wine and cook it all away, 1 minute. Add a few ladles of warm stock and let the rice absorb it, stirring occasionally. The risotto will take 22 minutes to cook. Add a ladle of broth as each addition is absorbed, until the risotto is starchy, creamy, and cooked to al dente. Add the peas when the risotto is just about al dente, the last minute or two. Add the cheese, mint, and parsley just before serving.

When the risotto is half cooked, 10 minutes from being done, drizzle the lamb chops with EVOO and arrange them on a slotted broiler pan. Place the chops under the hot broiler and cook for 8 to 10 minutes for medium rare. Place a tiny pan on the stove over medium heat. Add the remaining tablespoon of EVOO and the shallots to the pan. Cook the shallots for 2 minutes, then add the preserves and whisk them together with the balsamic vinegar and black pepper. Heat them to a bubble, then remove them from the heat and add the remaining tablespoon of butter. Whisk the butter into the sauce.

Season the risotto with salt to taste. Place a generous serving of risotto into shallow dinner plates. Arrange 2 chops on each plate alongside the risotto and drizzle the black cherry–black pepper glaze over the chops. Garnish the plates with extra sprigs of mint.

**And make sure you have
the following On Hand:**

Chicken stock • Butter •
EVOO • Onion • Garlic •
White wine • Frozen green
peas • Parmigiano-Reggiano
cheese • Flat-leaf parsley •
Shallot • Balsamic vinegar •
Cracked black pepper • Salt

Thai-Style Grilled Beef in Broth with a Lot o' Noodles (MYOTO)

Thai-style food made with ingredients available in any grocery store. If you're not into beef, try it with pork or chicken, instead.

4 SERVINGS

Salt

½ pound **thin pasta**, such as vermicelli

3-inch piece **fresh ginger**, peeled and grated

2 tablespoons **Worcestershire sauce** (eyeball it)

4 tablespoons **vegetable oil**

2 teaspoons **hot sauce** (eyeball it)

4 ½-inch-thick **shell steaks**

1 teaspoon **ground coriander**, ⅓ palmful

½ teaspoon **ground cumin** (eyeball it in your palm)

1 large **onion**, thinly sliced

4 **garlic cloves**, finely chopped

1 medium **carrot**, peeled and grated

2 **celery ribs**, thinly sliced

1 **jalapeño or serrano pepper**, seeded and finely chopped

12 **shiitake mushrooms**, stems removed and discarded, caps thinly sliced

Black pepper

5 cups **chicken stock**

¼ cup fresh **cilantro leaves**, chopped, a generous handful

¾ cup fresh **basil**, chopped, about 15 leaves

Juice of 1 lime

Preheat an outdoor grill or grill pan over high heat.

Bring a large pot of water with a tight-fitting lid to a boil over high heat to cook the pasta. Once it comes to a boil, add some salt and the pasta. Cook the pasta according to the package directions until it is al dente, drain, and run it under cold water to rinse off some of the starch. Let the noodles sit in the colander for a few minutes to dry off.

While the water is coming up to a boil, in a shallow dish combine half of the ginger, the Worcestershire sauce, 2 tablespoons of the vegetable oil, and the hot sauce. Add the shell steaks and let them marinate while you get everything else working.

Preheat a soup pot over medium-high heat with the remaining 2 table-spoons of vegetable oil, twice around the pan. Add the coriander and cumin and toast them for about 30 seconds, stirring constantly. Add the onions, garlic, carrots, celery, the remaining ginger, the jalapeño or serrano pepper, shiitake mushrooms, salt, and a little pepper; cook, stirring every now and then, for 3 to 4 minutes. Add the chicken stock and bring it up to a bubble; reduce the heat and then let it simmer for 10 to 15 minutes.

While the broth is cooking away, get the steaks cooking. Season the steaks with a little salt, transfer them to the hot grill, and cook on each side for about 2 minutes. Remove them from the grill and let them rest for a few minutes. Thinly slice the steaks on a sharp angle (this is always easier to do when you are using a sharp knife). Cut the thin slices in half.

Once the broth is simmering, add the cooked drained noodles, the cilantro, and basil. Reheat the noodles, 1 minute. Add the lime juice to the pot and then taste for seasoning; add salt and pepper accordingly. To serve, use kitchen tongs to transfer 4 servings of the noodles and veggies to soup bowls. Top each noodle pile with some of the grilled sliced steak, then ladle some of the broth over the top.

EXPRESS LANE SHOPPING LIST

❑ 3-inch piece fresh ginger
❑ 4 ½-inch-thick shell steaks, about 1½ pounds
❑ 1 jalapeño or serrano pepper
❑ 12 shiitake mushrooms
❑ 1 bunch fresh cilantro
❑ 1 bunch fresh basil

And make sure you have the following On Hand:

Salt • Thin long-cut pasta • Worcestershire • Vegetable oil • Hot sauce • Ground coriander • Ground cumin • Onion • Garlic • Carrot • Celery • Black pepper • Chicken stock • Lime

Spicy and Sweet Chicken and Couscous Pot with Minty Cilantro Sauce

Exotic, easy, and healthy, too, this simple dish is just delish.

4 SERVINGS

2½ cups **chicken stock**

½ cup **mango chutney**

Salt and **black pepper**

2 tablespoons **EVOO** (extra-virgin olive oil), twice around the pan

½ tablespoon **ground coriander**, ½ palmful

1 teaspoons **ground cumin**, ⅓ palmful

½ teaspoon **red pepper flakes** (eyeball it in your palm)

4 boneless, skinless **chicken breasts**, cut into large bite-size pieces

1 large **onion**, thinly sliced

1 red **bell pepper**, cored, seeded, and thinly sliced

3 **garlic cloves**, finely chopped

3-inch piece **fresh ginger**, peeled and grated

Zest and juice of 1 lemon

1½ cups plain **couscous**

½ cup **plain yogurt**

10 fresh **mint** leaves, from several sprigs

¼ cup fresh **cilantro leaves**, a generous handful

3 **scallions**, trimmed, coarsely chopped

Juice of 1 lime

In a sauce pot over medium-low heat, combine 2 cups of the chicken stock with the mango chutney and a little salt and pepper, bring it up to a bubble, and then turn down the heat to low to just keep warm.

Heat a large skillet with high sides or a soup pot over medium-high heat with the EVOO. Once the oil is hot, add the coriander, cumin, and red pepper flakes to the oil and "toast" the spices, stirring constantly for about 15 seconds. Add the chicken and toss it in the spices until well coated. Spread the chicken out in an even layer and season it with salt and pepper. Cook the chicken pieces for 2 minutes on each side to brown, then add the onions, red bell pepper, garlic, and three fourths of the grated ginger. Cook for about 3 minutes, stirring frequently. Add the remaining ½ cup of chicken stock and continue to cook until almost all of the liquids have evaporated, about 2 to 3 minutes.

Scoot the chicken and veggies to the sides of the skillet, creating a crater in the center of the pan. Add the chicken stock–chutney mixture and the lemon zest and juice, bring up to a bubble, and then add the couscous to the crater. Give the skillet a shake to get the couscous to settle into the liquids but still try to keep it in the crater. Use the back of a spoon to spread it out into the liquids if the shaking doesn't do the trick. Cover it with a tight-fitting lid or with a piece of aluminum foil (if you are using foil, really wrap the top of the pan; you need to hold in the steam) and then turn off the heat and let it sit for about 5 minutes to cook the couscous.

While the couscous is cooking with the chicken and the veggies, make the minty cilantro sauce. In a blender combine the yogurt, mint, cilantro, scallions, lime juice, the remaining grated ginger, and a small splash of water. Turn the blender on and puree until the mixture is smooth. If it doesn't get going right away, add another splash of water to get it moving. Season the sauce with a little salt and pepper.

To serve, with a fork mix the couscous with the chicken and veggies, serve up a couple of heaping spoonfuls in shallow bowls, and give each serving a generous drizzle of the minty cilantro sauce.

EXPRESS LANE SHOPPING LIST

- ❑ 1 jar mango chutney
- ❑ 4 boneless, skinless chicken breasts, 6 ounces each
- ❑ 1 red bell pepper
- ❑ 3-inch piece fresh ginger
- ❑ 1 8-ounce container plain yogurt
- ❑ 1 bunch fresh mint
- ❑ 1 bunch fresh cilantro
- ❑ 1 bunch scallions

And make sure you have the following On Hand:

Chicken stock • Salt and black pepper • EVOO • Ground coriander • Ground cumin • Red pepper flakes • Onion • Garlic • Lemon • Plain couscous • Lime

Steak Niçoise

Hey, why should tuna have all the fun? Try this even-heartier rendition.

4 SERVINGS

- 3 tablespoons **Worcestershire sauce** (eyeball it)
- 2 **garlic cloves**, finely chopped
- 2 teaspoons **hot sauce** (eyeball it)
- 7 tablespoons **EVOO** (extra-virgin olive oil)
  Black pepper
- 2 pounds **boneless shoulder** or top round steak
- 2 pounds white or red **boiling potatoes**, halved
  Salt
- 4 **eggs**
- 1 pound trimmed **fresh green beans**
- 2 large **shallots**, finely chopped
  A couple of **anchovy fillets**, finely chopped (optional)
- 1 heaping tablespoon **Dijon mustard**
- 3 tablespoons **red wine vinegar** (eyeball it)
- 1 tablespoon **capers**
- 6 cups **mixed greens**, multiple large handfuls
- 1 cup fresh **basil**, 20 leaves, chopped or torn
- ½ cup **pitted kalamata olives**
- ¼ cup fresh **flat-leaf parsley**, a generous handful, chopped
- 2 **vine-ripe tomatoes**, cut into 8 wedges each

> **TIDBIT**
> Many markets sell trimmed raw green beans in packages in the fresh produce department; if your market doesn't, just snap off the stem end of the beans.

Preheat the broiler and place the rack as in the highest position.

In a shallow dish, combine the Worcestershire sauce, garlic, hot sauce, 3 tablespoons of the EVOO, and a good amount of black pepper. Add the meat and coat it thoroughly. Let the meat hang out and marinate while you get the potatoes, eggs, and green beans going.

Place the halved potatoes in a pot. Cover them with water and bring them to a boil over high heat. When the water boils, add 2 big pinches of salt and boil the potatoes for 10 minutes, or until tender. Drain and spread them out on a cookie sheet to cool.

While the potatoes cook, place the eggs in a small saucepot and add enough water to cover. Bring them up to a simmer over high heat and then turn the heat off, cover them with a lid, and let them sit for 10 minutes. Drain the eggs, then aggressively shake the pan to crack the shells. Run the eggs under cold water until they cool down a little. Peel the eggs and then cut them into quarters.

Fill a large skillet with 1 inch of water, place it over high heat, and bring it up to a boil. Add a large pinch of salt and the green beans. Cook the green beans for 1 minute, drain, and run them under cold water to stop the cooking process.

Once the potatoes, eggs, and water for the beans are going, put the steak on a broiler pan, season it with some salt, and broil for 6 minutes per side. Remove it from the broiler and allow the meat to rest for 5 minutes, tented with a piece of aluminum foil.

For the dressing, in a mixing bowl combine the shallots, anchovies (if using), mustard, vinegar, and capers with some salt and pepper. In a slow steady stream, whisk in the remaining 4 tablespoons (¼ cup) of EVOO.

On a platter toss together the cooled green beans, mixed greens, basil, olives, and parsley. Arrange the quartered hard-boiled eggs, tomato wedges, and cooled potatoes around the platter. Slice the rested steak very thin, against the grain and on a slight angle, and arrange the steak slices on top of the greens. Drizzle the dressing over the entire salad.

EXPRESS LANE SHOPPING LIST

- ❑ 2 pounds boneless shoulder steak (or top round steak (marked London Broil)
- ❑ 1 pound green beans
- ❑ 1 large or 2 small sacks mixed greens
- ❑ 1 bunch fresh basil
- ❑ ½ pint pitted kalamata olives, or if you are feeling industrious get Niçoise olives, but you will have to pit them yourself
- ❑ 2 vine-ripe tomatoes

And make sure you have the following On Hand:

Worcestershire • Garlic • Hot sauce • EVOO • Black pepper • White or red boiling potatoes • Salt • Eggs • Shallots • Anchovy fillets (optional) • Dijon mustard • Red wine vinegar • Capers • Flat-leaf parsley

Smoky Chipotle–Chicken Corn Chowder with Salsa Salad

East Coast meets West Coast in this dish. Chowder plus Tex-Mex equals a really good idea in any direction!

4 SERVINGS

- 5 tablespoons **EVOO** (extra-virgin olive oil)
- 1 large **onion**, chopped
- 3 large **garlic cloves**, chopped
- 1 **chipotle chili in adobo**, chopped
- 2 **celery ribs**, finely chopped
- 1 teaspoon **ground coriander**, ⅓ handful
- ½ teaspoon **ground cumin** (eyeball it)
- **Salt** and **black pepper**
- 20 white or yellow **tortilla chips**, plus some for garnish
- 1 quart **chicken stock**
- 3 boneless, skinless **chicken breasts**, cut in half lengthwise, then cut into small bite-size pieces
- 2 10-ounce boxes **frozen corn kernels**
- **Juice of 2 limes**
- 1 tablespoon **Dijon mustard** (eyeball it)
- 2 ripe **Hass avocados**
- 1 pint **grape tomatoes**
- 2 tablespoons fresh **cilantro leaves**, a palmful, chopped
- 1 small head **romaine lettuce**, washed and coarsely chopped
- ½ small **red onion**, finely chopped
- ¼ cup fresh **flat-leaf parsley**, a generous handful, chopped

Preheat a soup pot over medium-high heat with 2 tablespoons of the EVOO, twice around the pan. Add the onions, garlic, chipotle, celery, coriander, cumin, and a little salt and pepper. Cook for about 3 minutes or until the onions are slightly tender, stirring frequently.

While the onions are cooking, in a food processor grind the tortilla chips until they are pretty fine. If you don't have a food processor, put the chips in a resealable plastic bag and smash them up using a rolling pin until you don't feel like doing it anymore. They might not be ground as fine as they would be in the machine, but it won't matter in the end. You need about 1 cup of ground chips; since different brands of chips come in different sizes, adjust the amount you grind accordingly. Add the ground chips to the onions, stir to combine, then add the chicken stock, bring it up to a bubble, and simmer for 8 to 10 minutes. Add the chicken and frozen corn and continue to cook it for 5 minutes, or until the chicken is cooked through.

While the soup is cooking, prepare the salsa salad. To make the dressing, in a small mixing bowl combine the juice of 1 lime, the mustard, and a little salt and pepper. In a slow steady stream whisk in the remaining 3 tablespoons of EVOO. Reserve the dressing.

Cut all around the circumference of the avocados, lengthwise and down to the pit. Twist and separate the halved fruit. Remove the pit with a spoon, then scoop the flesh out in one piece from both halves, chop it into bite-size pieces, and transfer it to a salad bowl. Cut the grape tomatoes in half and add them to the avocados along with the cilantro, chopped romaine lettuce, and chopped red onion. Pour the dressing over the salad and toss it to coat and combine.

If the soup becomes too thick, adjust it by adding a little more stock, and if it is too thin, let it continue to cook and reduce until it is to your liking. Taste and check for seasoning, adjust with a little salt and pepper, and if you want more heat, you have that hot sauce on hand, so use it. Add the parsley and serve the soup with the salsa salad alongside. Garnish each bowl of soup with a chip or two.

EXPRESS LANE SHOPPING LIST

- ❑ 1 sack white or yellow tortilla chips
- ❑ 3 boneless, skinless chicken breasts, 6 ounces each
- ❑ 2 ripe Hass avocados
- ❑ 1 pint grape tomatoes
- ❑ 1 bunch fresh cilantro
- ❑ 1 small head romaine lettuce
- ❑ 1 small red onion

And make sure you have the following On Hand:

EVOO • Onion • Garlic • Canned chipotle chili in adobo • Celery • Ground coriander • Ground cumin • Salt and black pepper • Chicken stock • Frozen corn kernels • Limes • Dijon mustard • Flat-leaf parsley

Rosemary Pork Chops with Balsamic Pan Gravy and Broccoli with Crispy Soppressata

Feel free to swap out the green vegetable for whatever looks good. My husband, John, loves salami and really all pork in general. The only thing he likes better is a meal like this one, which combines pork *and* crispy salami-topped side dishes!

4 SERVINGS

- 5 tablespoons **EVOO** (extra-virgin olive oil)
- 12 thin slices sweet or spicy **soppressata**, cut into thin strips (separate the strips after slicing)
- 4 **center-cut pork loin chops**, 1 inch thick

  Salt and **black pepper**
- 2 sprigs fresh **rosemary**, leaves stripped from the stem, then finely chopped
- 1 large head **broccoli**, tops cut into 1-inch florets, stem peeled of fibrous skin, then cut into bite-size pieces
- 4 **garlic cloves**, chopped
- 1 large **onion**, chopped
- 1½ cups **chicken stock**
- 3 tablespoons **balsamic vinegar** (eyeball it)
- 2 tablespoons **butter**
- 2 tablespoons chopped fresh **flat-leaf parsley**, a small handful

  Crusty bread

> NOTE: Genoa salami can be substituted for the soppressata.

Preheat a large nonstick skillet over medium heat with 1 tablespoon of the EVOO, once around the pan. Add the soppressata strips, spreading them evenly in the skillet, and cook, stirring frequently, until they are crispy, about 4 to 5 minutes.

While the soppressata is getting crispy, start the pork chops. Preheat a second skillet over medium-high heat with 2 tablespoons of the EVOO. Season the pork chops with salt, pepper, and the rosemary. Add the chops and cook for 5 minutes on each side.

Back to the soppressata: remove the crispy soppressata to a paper-towel-lined plate and reserve. Return the skillet to the heat with 1 tablespoon of the EVOO. Add the broccoli florets and the bite-size stem pieces, season them with pepper and just a little salt, spread the broccoli out evenly in the skillet, and try not to stir it for about 2 minutes in order for it to take on a little color. Once it is lightly colored, stir and add half of the garlic and half of the chopped onions. Continue to cook for about 2 minutes, then add $1/2$ cup of the chicken stock. Turn the heat down to medium, and continue to cook until the broccoli is nice and tender, about 5 minutes. If the skillet gets dry before the broccoli is tender, add another splash of either the chicken stock or water.

Once the pork chops have done their time in the skillet, transfer to a platter and loosely cover with foil. Return the pan to the heat and add the remaining tablespoon of EVOO and the remaining garlic and onions. Season with a little salt and pepper. Sauté the onions for 3 to 4 minutes, until they are nice and tender, stirring frequently. Add the balsamic vinegar; cook for about 30 seconds, then add the remaining 1 cup of chicken stock. Bring it up to a bubble and continue to cook for about 2 minutes, or until there is only about $1/2$ cup of liquid left in the skillet. Turn the heat off and add the butter and chopped parsley, stirring and shaking the pan until the butter has completely melted.

Distribute the broccoli among 4 serving plates and top each serving with a little of the crispy soppressata. Arrange a pork chop on each plate and drizzle it with the balsamic pan gravy. Serve with a big hunk of crunchy bread.

Thai Shrimp and Pork Balls over Coconut Curried Noodles

This dish is so good that if you ever share it with friends they'll each be calling you the next week for home delivery. Ask for a generous tip.

4 SERVINGS

Salt

1 pound of thin **long-cut pasta**

4 **scallions**, trimmed

3-inch piece **fresh ginger**, peeled and grated

1 **serrano** or **jalapeño pepper**, seeded and finely chopped

4 **garlic cloves**, 2 crushed, 2 chopped

4 tablespoons **tamari** (eyeball it)

¼ cup fresh **cilantro leaves**

1 cup fresh **basil**, 20 leaves, coarsely chopped or torn

Zest and juice of 1 lime

1 pound medium **shrimp**, shelled and deveined

1 pound **ground pork**

6 tablespoons **vegetable oil**

1 teaspoon **ground coriander**, ⅓ palmful

½ teaspoon **ground cumin** (eyeball it in your palm)

1 tablespoon **curry powder**, a palmful

1 medium **onion**, thinly sliced

1 small **carrot**, peeled and grated

1 large red **bell pepper**, cored, seeded, and thinly sliced

1 cup **chicken stock**

1 cup canned **unsweetened coconut milk**

Hot sauce (optional)

Place a large pot of water with a tight-fitting lid over high heat and bring it to a boil. Add some salt and the pasta and cook until al dente. Drain the pasta thoroughly and reserve.

While the water is coming up to a boil for the pasta, start the shrimp and pork balls. In the bowl of a food processor, combine the scallions, half of the grated ginger, half of the chopped serrano or jalapeño pepper, the garlic, 3 tablespoons of the tamari, half of the cilantro and basil, and the lime zest. Pulse for 30 seconds, scrape down the bowl, and then process 1 minute, or until finely ground. Add the shrimp and pork and process until the shrimp are ground into small pieces and the mixture is well combined but not so fine that it becomes a paste, about 1 minute.

Preheat a large nonstick skillet with 4 tablespoons of the oil. With wet palms, roll the shrimp-pork mixture into walnut-size balls and add to the hot skillet as you go. Don't move the balls until they are brown on one side, about 2 minutes. Turn the balls and continue to cook, browning on all sides until cooked through, about 3 to 4 minutes.

While the shrimp and pork balls and pasta are cooking, start the coconut curry sauce for the noodles. Preheat a large skillet or soup pot over medium heat with the remaining 2 tablespoons of oil. Add the coriander, cumin, and curry powder and toast the spices for about 30 seconds in the hot oil. Add the onions, carrot, bell pepper, the remaining ginger and serrano or jalapeño pepper, and the 2 chopped garlic cloves. Add a little more oil to the pan if it starts to look dry. Use a wooden spoon to scrape up any spices that might be sticking to the bottom of the pan. Cook the mixture, for about 3 minutes, stirring frequently.

Add the chicken stock, coconut milk, and the remaining tablespoon of tamari and bring it up to a bubble, then gently simmer for 5 minutes. Add the lime juice and taste and adjust for seasoning with either more tamari or a little salt. If you want a bit more spice, hit it with some hot sauce. Add the cooked drained noodles and the remaining cilantro and basil. Toss to combine. Divide the coconut curried noodles among 4 shallow bowls and top with the shrimp and pork balls.

EXPRESS LANE SHOPPING LIST

- ❑ 1 bunch scallions
- ❑ 3-inch piece fresh ginger
- ❑ 1 serrano or jalapeño pepper
- ❑ 1 bunch fresh cilantro
- ❑ 1 bunch fresh basil
- ❑ 1 pound medium shrimp
- ❑ 1 pound ground pork
- ❑ 1 large red bell pepper
- ❑ 1 15-ounce can unsweetened coconut milk

And make sure you have the following On Hand:

Salt • Long-cut pasta, the thinnest type you have • Garlic • Tamari • Lime • Vegetable oil • Ground coriander • Ground cumin • Curry powder • Onion • Carrot • Chicken stock • Hot sauce (optional)

Ginger-Orange Roasted Carrot Soup with Spicy Shrimp

Why roast the carrots? Well let me tell you, a roasted carrot will kick a boiled carrot's you know what, any day. That's why.

4 SERVINGS

- 1 pound **carrots**, peeled and sliced into ¼-inch-thick disks
- 5 tablespoons **EVOO** (extra-virgin olive oil), plus some for drizzling
- **Salt** and **black pepper**
- 1 **orange**
- 1 teaspoon **hot sauce** (eyeball it)
- 12 **large shrimp**, shelled, deveined, and butterflied (see Note)
- 2 medium **onions**, thinly sliced
- 2-inch piece **fresh ginger**, peeled and chopped
- 2 large **garlic cloves**, chopped
- 1 teaspoon **curry powder**, ⅓ palmful
- 1 quart **chicken stock**
- ¼ cup fresh **flat-leaf parsley**, a generous handful, chopped

NOTE: To butterfly the shrimp, using a paring knife run your knife lengthwise along where the vein was removed, just shy of cutting through. Once cooked, the shrimp will open like a butterfly and be able to sit upright in the soup.

Preheat the oven to 450°F.

Put the carrot disks on a cookie sheet, drizzle them with a little EVOO, and season them with salt and pepper. Toss the carrots around to make sure they are well coated. Spread in an even layer then roast them for 15 minutes, or until they are tender and the bottoms are browned. Stir the carrots at least twice while they roast so they cook evenly. Zest the orange and reserve.

In a shallow dish, combine the juice of half of the orange with the hot sauce, 2 tablespoons of the EVOO, and a little salt. Add the shrimp and toss to coat; set aside for a few minutes.

Preheat a soup pot over medium-high heat with 2 tablespoons of the EVOO, twice around the pan. Add the onions, ginger, garlic, curry powder, and salt and pepper to the pot and cook until the onions are tender and lightly colored, about 5 minutes, stirring frequently. If you find the onions are browning before they are getting tender, add a splash of water. Transfer the cooked onions to a blender or food processor, where they can wait for the carrots to finish roasting. Return the soup pot to the cooktop, add the chicken stock, and bring it up to a simmer.

When the carrots are roasted, transfer them to the blender or food processor where the onions are patiently waiting. Add a little ladle of the hot chicken stock and puree until the vegetables are smooth. Start by pulse-grinding the mixture to get it going and then let 'er rip. Add more hot stock, bit by bit, until it incorporates. Careful, sometimes when blending hot things the blender or food processor top is not tight enough and you can get splashed: put a kitchen towel over the lid for extra safety. (Hot carrot puree is not a home facial technique!) Add the carrot-onion puree to the bubbling stock and stir to combine, then let the soup gently simmer while you cook the shrimp.

Preheat a large skillet over medium-high heat with the remaining tablespoon of EVOO. Drain the shrimp and cook them on each side for 2 to 3 minutes, or until cooked through. Add the parsley and toss.

Check the soup consistency. If you want it thicker let it simmer a little bit longer; if you want it less thick, add a couple splashes of chicken stock to thin it out. Add the orange zest, stir it to combine, then taste and check for seasoning and adjust with salt and pepper.

Ladle some soup into shallow serving bowls and arrange 3 shrimp in the center of each bowl, standing up if you can manage it.

EXPRESS LANE
SHOPPING LIST

❑ 1 orange
❑ 12 large shrimp
❑ 2-inch piece fresh ginger

And make sure you have
the following On Hand:

Carrots • EVOO • Salt and
black pepper • Hot sauce
• Onions • Garlic • Curry
powder • Chicken stock •
Flat-leaf parsley

Curry Spiced Turkey Meatballs over Lemon Rice

This one is for Howard Stern. Howard loves the ground turkey. Here ya go, baby!

4 SERVINGS

3 tablespoons **EVOO** (extra-virgin olive oil)

1 tablespoon **ground coriander**

1 **celery rib**, finely chopped

1 small **carrot**, peeled and grated

5 **garlic cloves**, 1 crushed, the rest chopped

2 **lemons**

Salt and **black pepper**

1½ cups **white rice**

4½ cups **chicken stock**

1 package **ground turkey breast** or chicken breast

2 large **onions**, half of one grated, the rest thinly sliced

½ cup fresh **flat-leaf parsley**, a couple of handfuls, chopped

1 tablespoon **curry powder**, a palmful

½ teaspoon **ground cumin** (eyeball it in your palm)

3-inch piece **fresh ginger**, peeled and grated

2 tablespoons **butter**

1 **serrano pepper**, cut in half lengthwise

2 tablespoons **all-purpose flour**

¼ cup **mango chutney**

1 10-ounce box **frozen peas**

¼ cup fresh **cilantro leaves**, a generous handful, chopped

Heat a medium pot with a tight-fitting lid over medium-high heat. Add 1 tablespoon of the EVOO, once around the pan. Add ½ tablespoon of coriander, the celery, carrot, the crushed garlic clove, the zest of both lemons, and a little salt and pepper and cook, stirring, for about 1 minute. Add the rice and stir it to coat it in the oil. Add 2½ cups of the chicken stock and the juice of one of the lemons. Bring the stock to a boil, cover the pot, and reduce the heat to a simmer. Cook for 15 to 18 minutes, until the rice is tender.

In a mixing bowl, combine the ground meat, grated onion, half of the parsley, half of the chopped garlic, the curry powder, the remaining ½ tablespoon of coriander, the cumin, half of the grated ginger, and salt and pepper. Mix until just combined. Preheat a nonstick skillet over medium-high heat with the remaining 2 tablespoons of EVOO. Dip your hands in some water, then begin rolling small, bite-size balls, adding the balls to the pan as you roll them. Continue dipping and rolling until you have used up all the ground meat mixture. Let the meatballs get nice and brown before you turn them. Cook the balls for 10 to 12 minutes, shaking the pan occasionally to brown them equally on all sides.

Remove the balls from the skillet to a plate, return the skillet to the heat, and add the butter, sliced onion, the remaining chopped garlic, the rest of the grated ginger, the serrano pepper halves, and salt and pepper. Cook for about 3 minutes, until the onions are slightly tender, stirring frequently. Sprinkle the onions with the flour and continue to cook them for 1 minute. Whisk in the remaining 2 cups of chicken stock and bring the mixture up to a boil. Add the mango chutney and return the meatballs back to the skillet; cook for 2 to 3 minutes, add the peas, the remaining parsley, and the cilantro, and cook 1 more minute. Remove the serrano pepper from the sauce and discard. Divide the lemon rice among dinner plates and top it with some of the meatballs and sauce.

Classic French Bistro, Pardner
Salad Lyonnaise with a Rio Grande Kick in the Pants

I admit, toasting the bread cubes is the hardest part of this recipe for me. I burn a lot of bread, often. Use your favorite method for remembering: the rubber band around the wrist, a timer, or assign someone in the house to stand guard at the oven. (I use John.) It's always such a drag to have to do a "do over" when it comes to making croutons. It's humbling.

4 SERVINGS

- 1 large **garlic clove**, finely chopped
- ½ tablespoon **chili powder**, ½ palmful
  Salt
- ½ cup **EVOO** (extra-virgin olive oil)
- 5 thick slices **crusty bread**
- 6 **bacon slices**, coarsely chopped
- 2 **shallots**, chopped
- 1 small **jalapeño pepper**, seeded and finely chopped
- 2 tablespoons **white wine vinegar** (eyeball it)
  Zest and juice of 1 lime
  Freshly ground black pepper
- 1 tablespoon **Dijon mustard** (eyeball it)
- 8 **eggs**
- 2 heads **chicory**, washed and torn into bite-size pieces
- 2 heads **endive**, leaves pulled from the core
- ¼ cup fresh **cilantro leaves**, a generous handful, chopped
- ½ cup fresh **flat-leaf parsley**, a couple of handfuls, chopped

Preheat the oven to 325°F.

In a large mixing bowl, combine the garlic, chili powder, a couple of pinches of salt, and 3 tablespoons of the EVOO. Dice the bread into small cubes (think "crouton"). Add the bread cubes to the bowl and toss them to completely coat them with oil. Transfer the coated bread cubes to a cookie sheet and spread them out in an even layer. (Reserve the oiled bowl.) Toast in the oven until golden, about 8 minutes. Give the cookie sheet a good shake halfway through the cooking.

Fill a large skillet with warm water and bring it to a gentle simmer over medium-low heat.

Meanwhile, preheat a medium skillet over medium heat with 1 tablespoon of the EVOO, once around the pan. Add the bacon and cook until it is crisp, about 3 to 4 minutes, stirring frequently. Remove the crispy bacon to a paper-towel-lined plate. Return the pan to the heat and cook the shallots and jalapeño in the bacon drippings over medium heat for 3 to 4 minutes, until just tender. Whisk in 1 tablespoon of the vinegar, the lime juice and zest, some black pepper, and the mustard until well combined. While whisking, slowly drizzle in the remaining ¼ cup of EVOO until it is combined. Heads up: if you get one of those limes that are stingy with the juice, add another splash of vinegar to the dressing, or bump it up to 2 limes.

Pour the remaining tablespoon of vinegar into the simmering water. Crack an egg into a small bowl, without breaking the yolk. Gently pour the egg into the simmering water. Repeat with the remaining 7 eggs. Cook the eggs for about 2 minutes for runny yolks, or about 4 for solid yolks. Do not allow the water to boil—the bubbles are rough on the delicate eggs! Carefully remove the eggs with a slotted spoon to a towel-lined plate to drain.

While the eggs are poaching, tear the chicory into bite-size pieces and chop the endive into thin strips. Put the greens in the same bowl you tossed the bread in. Add the dressing, cilantro, parsley, chili croutons, and crispy bacon and toss well with tongs. Divide the salad among 4 plates and top each with 2 poached eggs. Season the salad with more salt and freshly ground black pepper.

EXPRESS LANE SHOPPING LIST

- ❏ 1 loaf crusty bread
- ❏ 1 small jalapeño pepper
- ❏ 2 heads chicory
- ❏ 2 heads endive
- ❏ 1 bunch fresh cilantro

And make sure you have the following On Hand:

Garlic • Chili powder • Salt • EVOO • Bacon • Shallots • White wine vinegar • Lime • Black pepper • Dijon mustard • Eggs • Flat-leaf parsley

Bacon and Creamy Ranch Chicken Burgers with Crispy Scallion "Sticks"

Wow! Is this one a looker!

4 SERVINGS

- 8 **bacon slices**
- 1 package **ground chicken breast**
- 2 **garlic cloves**, finely chopped
- ½ small **onion**, grated
- ¼ cup fresh **flat-leaf parsley**, a generous handful, chopped
- ¼ pound **dill havarti cheese**, cut into ¼-inch dice (see Note)
- 2 teaspoons **poultry seasoning**, ⅔ palmful
- 2 **lemons**
  Salt and **black pepper**
  Vegetable oil, for frying and for drizzling
- 2 cups **buttermilk**
- 1 teaspoon **paprika**, ⅓ palmful
  All-purpose flour, for dredging
- 16 to 18 **scallions**, trimmed of roots
- 4 sandwich-size **English muffins**, split
  Creamy Ranch dressing, for slathering toasted muffins
- 1 **beefsteak tomato**, cut into 8 slices

> NOTE: The colder the cheese, the easier it is to dice. Pop it in the freezer while you prep everything else and you will find that dicing it will be a breeze.

Cook the bacon in a large nonstick skillet over medium-high heat until it is crisp.

While the bacon cooks, in a large bowl combine the ground chicken, garlic, onion, parsley, dill havarti chunks, poultry seasoning, the zest and juice of $\frac{1}{2}$ lemon, salt, and pepper. Divide the mixture into 4 equal mounds, then form the meat into large, thin patties, about 1 inch thick. Drizzle them with vegetable oil to coat.

Remove the crispy bacon from the skillet to a paper-towel-lined plate and reserve. Wipe the excess grease from the skillet and return it to the cooktop over medium-high heat, add the burgers to the skillet, and cook them for 5 to 6 minutes on each side, or until they are cooked through.

While the burgers are cooking, put together the scallion "sticks." Heat $1\frac{1}{2}$ inches of the vegetable oil in a deep-sided skillet over medium heat. In a wide mixing bowl, combine the buttermilk, paprika, and the zest of the remaining $1\frac{1}{2}$ lemons. Place the flour in a second wide mixing bowl. Before you go at it, take one of the scallions and hold it up next to the skillet containing the heating oil. If needed, trim off some of the green tops to allow it to fit in the skillet easily.

Line a plate with a few paper towels and set it near the stovetop. Add a 1-inch cube of bread to the hot oil. If it turns deep golden brown in color after a count of 40, the oil is ready. If the bread cube browns too quickly, turn down the heat and wait a few minutes for it to cool.

Working in 2 to 3 batches, dip some of the scallions in the buttermilk, then into the flour, coating thoroughly. Put them back into the buttermilk and then into the flour again. Fry the coated scallions into the hot oil for about 1 minute on each side, or until golden brown. Transfer to the paper-towel-lined plate and immediately season them with a little salt. Repeat the process until all the scallion "sticks" are fried up.

Toast the English muffins and slather both sides with the Ranch dressing. Arrange the cooked Ranch burgers on the English muffin bottoms, top each burger with 2 slices of the crispy bacon and 2 slices of tomato, and finish them with the English muffin tops. Serve them alongside the crispy scallion "sticks."

Montalcino Chicken with Figs and Buttered Gnocchi with Nutmeg

Montalcino, Italy, is the city I married in. I will make this dish for John every September 24, for our wedding anniversary. The way to anyone's heart, forever and ever, is through their stomach! This is *not* your average chicken dinner.

4 SERVINGS

- ¼ cup **EVOO** (extra-virgin olive oil), 4 times around the pan
- ⅓ pound thick-cut (¼-inch thick) **pancetta**, cut into sticks (see Notes)
- 2 pounds boneless, skinless **chicken**, **breasts and thighs**, cut into large chunks
- **Salt** and **black pepper**
- **Flour**, for dredging
- 1 large **onion**, thinly sliced
- 4 **garlic cloves**, crushed
- 14 to 16 **dried black mission figs**, quartered
- ⅓ bottle **Rosso di Montalcino wine** (eyeball it)
- 1 cup **chicken stock** plus up to ½ cup more if needed
- ¼ cup fresh **flat-leaf parsley**, a generous handful, chopped
- **Zest of 1 lemon**
- 1 tablespoon chopped fresh **thyme**, 4 sprigs
- 1 12- to 16-ounce package fresh or frozen **gnocchi**
- 3 tablespoons **butter**
- ¼ teaspoon freshly **grated nutmeg** (eyeball it)
- 3 tablespoons chopped or snipped **chives**, 10 blades

> **NOTE:** Look for plump, tender dried figs in the bulk section of the market or buy the figs in packages. Check for tough stem tops and trim them off if necessary.
>
> This dish uses Rosso di Montalcino wine (an affordable, younger version of Brunello—I call it "Baby Brunello") but you can substitute any dry red wine you like from your On Hand supply.

Place a pot of water on the stove to boil for the gnocchi.

Heat a deep skillet over medium-high heat. Add the EVOO and the pancetta. Brown the pancetta, 3 to 4 minutes, then remove it with a slotted spoon and reserve.

While the pancetta browns, season the chicken chunks with salt and pepper and dredge them in a little flour. After removing the pancetta from the pan, add the chicken. Brown the pieces for a few minutes on each side over high heat, then scoot the meat to the edges of the pan and add the onions, garlic, and figs. Sauté 5 minutes, combine the chicken with the onions and figs, then add the wine and cook it down for 5 minutes or so until only about $1/3$ cup of liquid remains. Add 1 cup of the chicken stock, the parsley, lemon zest, and thyme to the chicken and stir to combine. Reduce the heat to a simmer and cook for another 10 minutes, while you make the gnocchi.

Add salt and gnocchi to the boiling water and cook them according to package directions, 4 minutes for fresh gnocchi, 6 minutes for frozen. Drain. Heat a medium nonstick skillet over medium-low heat. Melt the butter and brown it. Add the drained gnocchi to the browned butter. Raise the heat to medium high and lightly brown the gnocchi. Season the gnocchi with salt, pepper, and nutmeg, turn to coat, and add the chives, toss, and remove from the heat.

Adjust the seasonings on the chicken with figs. If you would like a little more sauce, add another half cup of stock to the pan. Serve the chicken and figs in shallow dishes, the gnocchi piled in the center of the bowl on top of the chicken. Garnish it with the crisp pancetta sticks.

Lemony Salmon Fillets with Asparagus, Sweet Beet Sauce, and Lemon-Thyme Rice

This is salmon with some soul. It's groovy.

4 SERVINGS

- 6 tablespoons **EVOO** (extra-virgin olive oil)
- 4 **garlic cloves**, 1 crushed, 3 finely chopped
  Zest and juice of 1 lemon
- 1 teaspoon **dried thyme**, 1/3 palmful
  Salt and **black pepper**
- 1½ cups **white rice**
- 3 cups **chicken stock**
- 4 **salmon fillets**
- 1 pound pencil-thin **asparagus**, tough ends trimmed, spears cut into 2-inch pieces
- 1 softball-size **red beet**
- 1 small **onion**, chopped
- ½ cup **white wine**
- 1 cup fresh **basil**, 20 leaves, chopped or torn
- 2 tablespoons cold **butter**
- ¼ cup fresh **flat-leaf parsley**, a generous handful, chopped

Heat a medium pot with a tight-fitting lid over medium-high heat. Add 1 tablespoon of the EVOO, once around the pan. Add the crushed garlic clove, the lemon zest, thyme, and a little salt and pepper and cook, stirring, for about 1 minute. Add the rice and stir it to coat it in the oil. Add 2½ cups of the chicken stock and bring to a boil, then cover the pot and reduce the heat to a simmer. Cook for 15 to 18 minutes, until the rice is tender.

In a shallow dish, combine the lemon juice, 1 tablespoon of the EVOO, and about ½ teaspoon of freshly ground black pepper. Add the salmon fillets and turn them around in the mixture until all the fillets are completely coated. Let the salmon sit while you prepare the beets and get the asparagus going.

Fill a large skillet with about a ½ inch of water. Place the skillet over high heat with a lid or some aluminum foil on top to bring it up to a boil faster. Once it is boiling, add a little salt and the trimmed asparagus. If you have pencil-thin asparagus about 2 minutes will do the trick; if you have thick asparagus then 3 to 4 minutes. You want them to be tender but to remain bright green and keep a bite to them. Once cooked, drain and run them under cold water to stop the cooking. Reserve the asparagus.

While the asparagus is cooking, with a paring knife, peel the skin from the beet. You might want to place some paper towels on your cutting board to avoid beet-juice stains. Once the beet is peeled give your knife, your cutting board, and the peeled beet a rinse to make it a no-stray-grit zone. Using the large hole side of a box grater, grate the beet over a plate. Or, use the grating attachment on your food processor. (I can't find mine.)

Preheat a nonstick skillet over medium high with 2 tablespoons of the EVOO. Remove the salmon from the lemon mixture and season it with a little salt. Add the salmon to the hot skillet and cook it on each side for 3 to 4 minutes, or until just cooked through.

(continued on next page)

EXPRESS LANE SHOPPING LIST

☐ **4 salmon fillets, 6 ounces each**

☐ **1 pound pencil-thin asparagus**

☐ **1 softball-size red beet**

☐ **1 bunch fresh basil**

And make sure you have the following On Hand:

EVOO • Garlic • Lemon • Dried thyme • Salt and black pepper • White rice • Chicken stock • Onion • White wine • Butter • Flat-leaf parsley

While the salmon is cooking, return the skillet you cooked the asparagus in to the stove over medium-high heat, add the remaining 2 tablespoons of EVOO, and when the oil is hot add the grated beets, chopped garlic, and onions. Season with a little salt and pepper. Cook for about 4 to 5 minutes, or until the beets are sneaking up on getting tender, stirring frequently. Add the white wine and cook for 1 minute. Add the remaining ½ cup of chicken stock and bring it up to a bubble, then simmer for 2 to 3 minutes, or until you only have about ½ cup of liquids left in the skillet. Add the reserved cooked asparagus and heat through. Turn the heat off and add the basil and the butter, then stir it until the butter melts.

Add the chopped parsley to the rice. Using a fork, fluff the rice. While you are fluffing, keep your eyes peeled for the clove of garlic, fish it out, and discard.

To serve, arrange the salmon fillets on 4 serving plates and top them with some of the beet sauce and asparagus. Serve the rice alongside.

INDEX

EXPRESS LANE SHOPPING LIST

PRODUCE

_____
_____
_____

MEAT COUNTER

_____
_____
_____

DAIRY

_____
_____
_____

FREEZER CASE

_____
_____
_____

BAKERY

_____
_____
_____

**CANNED GOODS /
NONPERISHABLE**

_____
_____
_____

OTHER

_____
_____
_____

**ON-HAND ITEMS TO
REPLENISH**

_____
_____
_____

EXPRESS LANE SHOPPING LIST

PRODUCE

_____
_____
_____

MEAT COUNTER

_____
_____
_____

DAIRY

_____
_____
_____

FREEZER CASE

_____
_____
_____

BAKERY

_____
_____
_____

**CANNED GOODS /
NONPERISHABLE**

_____
_____
_____

OTHER

_____
_____
_____

**ON-HAND ITEMS TO
REPLENISH**

_____
_____
_____

EXPRESS LANE SHOPPING LIST

PRODUCE

_____
_____
_____

MEAT COUNTER

_____
_____
_____

DAIRY

_____
_____
_____

FREEZER CASE

_____
_____
_____

BAKERY

_____
_____
_____

**CANNED GOODS /
NONPERISHABLE**

_____
_____
_____

OTHER

_____
_____
_____

**ON-HAND ITEMS TO
REPLENISH**

_____
_____
_____

EXPRESS LANE
SHOPPING LIST

PRODUCE

_____
_____
_____

MEAT COUNTER

_____
_____
_____

DAIRY

_____
_____
_____

FREEZER CASE

_____
_____
_____

BAKERY

_____
_____
_____

**CANNED GOODS /
NONPERISHABLE**

_____
_____
_____

OTHER

_____
_____
_____

**ON-HAND ITEMS TO
REPLENISH**

_____
_____
_____

EXPRESS LANE
SHOPPING LIST

PRODUCE

_____
_____
_____

MEAT COUNTER

_____
_____
_____

DAIRY

_____
_____
_____

FREEZER CASE

_____
_____
_____

BAKERY

_____
_____
_____

**CANNED GOODS /
NONPERISHABLE**

_____
_____
_____

OTHER

_____
_____
_____

**ON-HAND ITEMS TO
REPLENISH**

_____
_____
_____

EXPRESS LANE
SHOPPING LIST

PRODUCE

_____
_____
_____

MEAT COUNTER

_____
_____
_____

DAIRY

_____
_____
_____

FREEZER CASE

_____
_____
_____

BAKERY

_____
_____
_____

**CANNED GOODS /
NONPERISHABLE**

_____
_____
_____

OTHER

_____
_____
_____

**ON-HAND ITEMS TO
REPLENISH**

_____
_____
_____

EXPRESS LANE
SHOPPING LIST

PRODUCE

MEAT COUNTER

DAIRY

FREEZER CASE

BAKERY

**CANNED GOODS /
NONPERISHABLE**

OTHER

**ON-HAND ITEMS TO
REPLENISH**

EXPRESS LANE
SHOPPING LIST

PRODUCE

MEAT COUNTER

DAIRY

FREEZER CASE

BAKERY

**CANNED GOODS /
NONPERISHABLE**

OTHER

**ON-HAND ITEMS TO
REPLENISH**

EXPRESS LANE
SHOPPING LIST

PRODUCE

MEAT COUNTER

DAIRY

FREEZER CASE

BAKERY

**CANNED GOODS /
NONPERISHABLE**

OTHER

**ON-HAND ITEMS TO
REPLENISH**

RACHAEL'S ON A ROLL!

SESN CAPERS
MCC CEL SALT
ORCHARD FIGS
THOMAS ISTR
HELLMAN MAYO
GOYA CAPER
VALUED CUSTOMER
TAX
***** BALANCE
Cash
CHANGE
OTAL NUMBER OF ITEM